Specially Designed Instruction

In engaging, accessible chapters, expert teacher and author Anne M. Beninghof lays out a road map for providing specially designed instruction in any classroom. This book equips you with the answers to the most frequently asked questions around incorporating special education services into the general classroom – What is SDI? Who is responsible? How do we make it happen?

Focused on creating an effective planning process that you and your team can follow to develop specially designed instruction, this toolkit includes dozens of practical examples, worksheets, and prep tools to ensure readers walk away with a thorough understanding and ready-to-use ideas. Whether you have years of experience working with students with disabilities or are new to the profession, this critical guide provides effective strategies for every classroom.

Anne M. Beninghof is an internationally recognized special educator, consultant and trainer, focusing on creative, practical solutions for more effectively including students with diverse learning needs in general education classrooms.

Other Eye On Education Books
Available From Routledge
(www.routledge.com/k-12)

Specially Designed Instruction

Increasing Success for Students with Disabilities

Anne M. Beninghof

Routledge
Taylor & Francis Group

NEW YORK AND LONDON

First published 2022
by Routledge
605 Third Avenue, New York, NY 10158

and by Routledge
2 Park Square, Milton Park, Abingdon, Oxon, OX14 4RN

Routledge is an imprint of the Taylor & Francis Group, an informa business

Library of Congress Cataloging-in-Publication Data
Names: Beninghof, Anne M., author.
Title: Specially designed instruction in every classroom : increasing
  success for students with disabilities / Anne M. Beninghof.
Description: New York, NY : Routledge, 2021. | Includes bibliographical
  references. |
Identifiers: LCCN 2021007487 (print) | LCCN 2021007488 (ebook) | ISBN
  9780367622572 (hardback) | ISBN 9780367616120 (paperback) | ISBN
  9781003108580 (ebook)
Subjects: LCSH: Children with disabilities--Education--United States. |
  Mainstreaming in education--United States. | Individualized
  instruction--United States. | Classroom management--United States.
Classification: LCC LC4031 .B423 2021 (print) | LCC LC4031 (ebook) | DDC
  371.9--dc23
LC record available at https://lccn.loc.gov/2021007487
LC ebook record available at https://lccn.loc.gov/2021007488

ISBN: 978-0-367-62257-2 (hbk)
ISBN: 978-0-367-61612-0 (pbk)
ISBN: 978-1-003-10858-0 (ebk)

Typeset in Palatino
by SPi Technologies India Pvt Ltd (Straive)

Contents

Figures and Tables

Figures

Tables

Author's Note

Hanging on the wall above my desk is a framed one-dollar bill – the first dollar I ever earned as an author. The year was 1994 and my book *Ideas for Inclusion: The Classroom Teacher's Guide* was available to help teachers make inclusive environments a reality for students with disabilities. For more than 30 years I have been an advocate for inclusive practices, believing that the very best opportunities for all students are found in the general education setting.

Because of my inclusive philosophy, most of the examples in this book occur in general education classrooms. However, specially designed instruction, the topic of this book, can take place in inclusive settings as well as separate, self-contained classrooms and facilities. I have described several examples taken from separate settings, but encourage readers to continually seek solutions that will make it possible for all students to be successfully taught alongside their non-disabled peers.

1

Introduction

My favorite pair of shoes were an olive-green pair of pumps with two-inch heels and a bit of bling on the front. Not only did they look great, they felt great. I could stand in them for hours without any distracting aches and pains, until all of a sudden – I couldn't. One day the ball of my foot complained with a quiet moan, but by the second day it was no longer being shy. Even in my well-worn running shoes, the pain was causing me to limp. After reading several blog posts, I decided that new running shoes would do the trick, so I visited a local shop known for their fitting expertise and walked away with a hefty credit card bill and a new pair of shoes.

No luck. It was time to break down and visit a podiatrist. First it was a cortisone injection, followed by kinesio tape and custom-designed orthotics. While the intensity of the pain diminished over the next few months, I still wasn't pain free nor was I able to return to running and cycling. Finally, I asked for a referral to a physical therapist specializing in foot injuries in athletes.

Misty did a thorough assessment of my feet, my stance and my walking and running technique. She showed me video of my foot moving through space, landing and lifting off again, all the while instructing me on the mechanics of the movement. She modeled, assisted and coached me through the changes I needed to make, reducing her supports until I was able to be independently successful. She also gave me a full course on shoe selection and fit so that I would not continue to purchase shoes that were a mismatch.

Misty specially designed her therapy so that my unique needs and goals were addressed. Twenty years later, I am still running and have a closet full of shoes that bring me joy!

Whether it is foot problems (like me), career counseling, parenting dilemmas or Marie Kondo decluttering, most of us have had an experience where we know we need help, but the simple strategies or tools that work for others don't work for us. We've read the advice columns, made some attempts and are still struggling, so, with hopes, we turn to the experts.

Students with disabilities need experts in specially designed instruction (SDI). Fortunately, special education teachers are primed to offer them this expertise. Moving beyond simple accommodations, specialists can provide intensive, individualized assessment and instruction that leads to independence and transfer. In the past, SDI may have been incorporated in alternate curricula that special education teachers were trained to implement. With the move to more inclusive settings and an expectation of access to general education curricula and standards, we need to find efficient and effective ways to integrate specially designed instruction into mainstream settings.

This book will provide you with dozens of practical ideas for accomplishing this. Whether you are working by yourself or in partnership with other educators, there are ideas for you. Whether you have abundant planning time or hardly any, there are ideas for you. Whether you have years of experience working with students with disabilities or are new to the profession, there are dozens of ideas that will work for you!

Part I, Envisioning SDI, includes clear examples of SDI and delves deeply into the meaning of the term. It provides a list of guiding elements to help you know when something is or isn't SDI, with opportunities to practice your analytical skills. It also explores how team members can work together to maximize their talents, with a variety of concrete recommendations.

Part II, Planning for SDI, includes chapters describing the seven-step process for creating SDI. Each chapter will provide examples and application opportunities so that you can build your comfort and skill as you progress through them.

Part III, Fulfilling the Promise of SDI, includes recommendations for implementation and assessment, with time-saving tips on data collection. A chapter on leadership synthesizes all of the previous information into ideas for school or district-wide implementation and sustainability.

Following the conclusion is an appendix filled with even more SDI examples, from various grades and content areas. Be prepared with sticky notes to flag the strategies you want to use right away!

Part I
Envisioning Specially Designed Instruction

Microsoft's 7000-square-foot Envisioning Center is located in Richmond, Washington. Inside this state-of-the-art facility, their envisioning team designs innovative solutions and prototypes for a wide range of known and unanticipated problems. Central to their process is the use of a "fluid framework" – a way of breaking down larger structures into modular components to make them more manageable. (Think Legos on steroids.) Envisioning teams imagine the future they want and then go about the business of creating it.

In order to have the best specially designed instruction for students with disabilities, we need to begin with imagining it. What does it look like? What is the foundational framework and how might we break this down so that the pieces are manageable? How can individual team members help to build a customized version for each unique student? While educators may not have a 7000-square-foot innovation facility, we have research and expertise that is just as valuable an asset to the process. So, let's get ready to deliver students to a promising future.

2

Specially Designed Instruction in Action

Mrs. Adams is a veteran general education teacher with a passion for working with students in low-income communities. The population at her school is very diverse, representing a number of cultures and languages, with class sizes that have been growing each year. Although crowded, her classroom is colorful and bursts with creative warmth, welcoming all students to be on the learning journey together. Mrs. Adams believes that students with disabilities should be included in general education classrooms, having a mindset of possibility and success. Her school is headed in an inclusive direction, but not fully there yet.

Mrs. Dominguez has always wanted to be a teacher. As a teenager she volunteered at a summer camp for students with disabilities, decided to pursue a degree in special education and then landed her first professional teaching job at a private school for students with significant disabilities. After a few years she craved a more inclusive philosophy and accepted a job at her neighborhood public elementary school. While the initial assignment was in a special education classroom, she hoped to move toward more inclusive practices. She worked to establish herself as "go-to" for general education teachers who had questions about executive function and reading disorders. Mrs. Adams reached out to Mrs. Dominguez several times, asking to brainstorm teaching ideas for some of her students with more unique needs.

Getting Started

The two teachers developed a conversational chemistry, enjoying the process of creating solutions together. Akin to the rituals of courting, they began to have discussions about how they might work more closely together through co-teaching. Honesty and vulnerability were key elements of their planning. Who would be responsible for behavior? What were their weaknesses and strengths? How would they decide what to do if they disagreed? After several conversations, they approached the building leadership to share their vision of providing special education services within the general education setting. After receiving administrative blessing, they were off and running. They spent the spring semester holding Individualized Education Plan (IEP) meetings, making team decisions about student placements, arranging schedules for the next school year and discussing the details of shared ownership.

Like all marriages or collaborative partnerships, there were some rough patches. Lessons that looked good on paper didn't always turn out that way. Students who appeared to be comfortable in the classroom had an off day and couldn't self-regulate. Occasionally, quiz scores showed that most of the students didn't get "it," even though they seemed to love the lesson. These rough patches smoothed out as the year progressed and both teachers developed a deeper understanding of how to integrate specially designed instruction into their lessons.

Percolating

One morning, Mrs. Dominguez opened her email to find a message from Mrs. Adams:

> "Heads up. I think we need something different for next week's ELA unit. The learning target in the curriculum is *I can use text evidence to support my claim* and I'm sure several will struggle with the standard approach to teaching this. Can you percolate on it a bit before our planning meeting?"

Mrs. Dominguez's commute time often provides her with the quiet time she needs to reflect on instruction and problem solve. She considers students' IEP goals and knows that several have literacy goals related to text evidence, persuasive writing and adding detail. She also tries to imagine and predict what might be difficult about this target. Some students will want to simply copy and paste any piece of text evidence, without really assessing its value. An "aha" moment occurs for her. Perhaps the learning target should be tweaked to read *"I can evaluate and select the best text evidence to support my claim."* By changing the verb from use to evaluate, they might avoid thoughtless click and paste, and instead develop the higher-level skills of evaluation.

Once Mrs. Dominguez arrives at school, she sends a brief message to Mrs. Adams to see if she is OK with tweaking the target language, and then immerses herself in the day-to-day responsibilities of a special educator. Even within her busy schedule of creating and serving up instruction that nurtures students, she finds brief moments when she thinks, "How do I evaluate text evidence?" This metacognitive awareness allows the question to simmer, transforming from its initial, simple ingredient to something more robust. Mrs. Dominguez has realized that at a subconscious level she asks herself a series of questions that help her evaluate which text passages to cite. She has identified her own metacognitive process and shifts to strategizing about how to teach it to their students, especially those with disabilities.

Planning Meeting

Planning time between Mrs. Adams and Mrs. Dominguez is highly structured. While they would love to talk about families and hobbies, they realized early on that in order to accomplish effective lesson planning for the week, they needed an agenda and norms that would keep them on track. If they stick to them, they can plan a lesson that includes specially designed instruction in about ten minutes, with a few follow-up tasks that are divided. They get right to work.

MRS. ADAMS: Did you manage to think of any ideas about our text evidence learning target?

MRS. DOMINGUEZ: I realized that I have four questions that I use, unconsciously, to evaluate evidence. I thought we could put them into a prioritized order and teach the process, maybe with a flow chart.

The partners quickly sketch out a flow chart that will organize information for the learners. Mrs. Dominguez volunteers to finalize it and print it for students. Next the teachers consider how to make it universally accessible.

MRS. DOMINGUEZ: I'd like to get students moving, so I thought we could create one of our floor mats of this flowchart. Students could walk through the process as they consider sample evidence.

These teachers have had success with this kinesthetic floor mat strategy in the past, so on a trip to a discount store Mrs. Adams had picked up five inexpensive shower curtain liners to use throughout the year. She grabs a new shower curtain liner from her cupboard and volunteers to make two so that they can split the class in half.

MRS. ADAMS: I think we might have a few students who will struggle with the meaning of words like "relevant" and "expandable." Could you do a pre-teach group for three minutes while I get the other students organized and reseated for their later group assignments?

MRS. DOMINGUEZ: Yes, and I think if I created an "expert sheet" with scaffolds built in, we could call these students our "experts" for the lesson, so they won't feel stigmatized.

By adding pre-teaching related to vocabulary, the partners are recognizing the needs of a few students for additional support. The specialized instruction in this small group can be tailored to address IEP or language goals and set students up for success. In addition, calling them "experts" reminds the whole class of the value of learning from peers.

Finally, the partners decide on a retrieval practice closing activity. Students will be provided a blank flow chart and be asked to try to retrieve the steps independently, before comparing with a peer.

Lesson Plan

Their lesson plan is sketched out (see Figures 2.1 and 2.2) and they move on to discussing the next targets in their instructional week.

Mrs. Dominguez is pleased with how the lesson goes, but intuitively knows that some of the students with IEPs will need more extensive practice with the process. She opens the online lesson planning document that she shares with Mrs. Adams and looks for lessons where it might be possible to reteach this process. Using the editing and commenting tools, she suggests adding small-group time into a few lessons, assigning herself to the task of revisiting their process for evaluating and choosing text evidence. A small group will provide her with a clearer sense of each student's progress and the time to customize her instruction to their needs. If her data don't show significant enough growth with related IEP goals, she will brainstorm with her partner about other ways to weave direct instruction into their class.

Learning Target: I can evaluate and choose the best text evidence to support my claim.
Questions to Support Target: What are we working on today? How do you choose evidence?
Assessment Plan: Teacher observation, writing samples, retrieval practice same day, next day and next week, data on related IEP goals

Activator Pre-teach flow chart to "expert group." Claim on board –"The most important reason to save the Everglades is so that the residents canhave clean drinking water." Each student will get a piece of evidence. Have them scrunch it and toss it at the board. Discuss how throwing evidence at something doesn't make it stick –instead we have to thoughtfully choose and place. T-P-S –What do you know about choosing evidence? Share out and capture on board. **Body of Lesson** Teachers will model flow chart on Hop/Step Mat with sample evidence. Break into two small mixed-readiness groups. Each group will have a Hop/Step Mat. Each student will havea paper copy of the flow chart and can take notes on it to help them understand each step. For example, next to "Relevant?" they might add a synonym. Students will take turns walking through the flow chart on the Hop/Step Curtain with their given piece of evidence to evaluate whether it should be used. "Expert" peers will ask questions. Students will justify their thinking. **Closure** Students will close eyes and retrieve/visualize the steps to evaluate evidence, then fill in blank flow chart.	**How will we challenge?** Complexity is inherent in evaluation task. Some students will be given more challenging pieces of evidence to evaluate. If teachers feel these students are ready, they can be sent off to independent writing early. **How will we support?** Flow chart for scaffolding –"expert version" for some Pre-teach group of "experts" Talk stems Hop/Step Mat Peer support Conferencing with specialist Retrieval practice for closure

Figure 2.1 Evaluating Text Evidence Lesson Plan

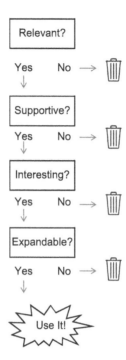

Figure 2.2 Evaluating Text Evidence Flowchart

To Sum Up

◆ As a special education teacher, Mrs. Dominguez' role is focused on the students with IEP goals, while the general education teacher, Mrs. Adams, brings her content expertise to the table.

◆ Mrs. Dominguez looked for ways to adapt and enrich the instruction, rather than just offering accommodations. Small-group instruction may be necessary to provide the intensity of individualized instruction that students with disabilities need.

◆ When the special education teacher was able to integrate her expertise into the whole-group lesson, all students benefited. Students with IEPs received specially designed instruction, while other students received incidental benefit.

Reflection Questions

- ◆ How is this vignette similar or different to your own teaching experiences?
- ◆ What structures and support need to be in place in order to embrace SDI and inclusive practices in your classroom or school?
- ◆ What might you like to change about your own practices? Why?

Try This

- ◆ Do a quick internet search for lesson plan templates. See if there are any components that appeal to you, especially for planning lessons that incorporate specially designed instruction into an inclusive classroom.

3

The What and Why of SDI

A recent review of various special education teacher job postings found an average of 17 different responsibilities listed, followed by the ever-popular "and any other duties assigned by the principal." A widespread meme on the internet claims "I'm called a special education teacher only because Full-Time, Multi-Tasking Ninja is not an actual job title." This is what it can feel like to be a special educator. High caseloads of students from various grade levels, with differing disabilities, and a handful of collaborative partners with wide-ranging personalities – all add up to an exciting, never-a-dull-moment work life that can also be overwhelming and confusing. Fortunately, specially designed instruction provides specialists with clarity of purpose.

What Is SDI?

Included in the federal definition of special education (34 CFR 300.39(b)(3)), specially designed instruction (SDI) is described as

> adapting, as appropriate to the needs of an eligible child under Part B of the IDEA, the content, methodology, or delivery of instruction to address the unique needs of the child that result from the child's disability and to ensure access of the child to the general curriculum, so that the child can meet the educational standards within the jurisdiction of the public agency that apply to all children.

SDI charges special educators with one or more of these three tasks, or three "whats":

1   To adapt content

When a student with an IEP is struggling with the content of the general education curriculum, the specialist looks for ways to adapt it. Would an alternate text be more effective? Would changing the order of the content work better? Are there sections of the content that could be eliminated so that more time is available to focus on key concepts? Does the student need lower-level standards with commensurate content in order to be successful? These are the types of questions that special educators ask themselves, all while keeping in mind the unique needs of each child on their caseload. In some cases, students may need expanded core curriculum to address compensatory skills such as using braille, mobility training, learning sign language or self-advocacy. Adding these content pieces would be considered SDI.

For busy educators, it can be tempting to adapt by simply lowering the content level. However, as we'll see in the section on the three purposes of SDI, this should not be the "go-to" approach. Years of low expectations have resulted in terrible outcomes for students with disabilities. Most students with disabilities will not need adapted content in order to be successful. Instead, they need changes to how they are being taught, rather than what they are being taught. The curriculum and methodology needs to be designed and adapted to meet their individual needs while maintaining enough rigor that gaps can be closed. Additionally, let's not forget that the word "adapt" might even mean that a student needs enriched content to avoid boredom related behaviors. Be very wary of the tendency to lower expectations.

2   To adapt methodology

Adapting methodology is the most common form of specially designed instruction. By examining a student's history and evaluation results, we can see that the general education methods are not working well enough for the child. This is not an indication of poor teaching! General education practices work for approximately 85% of the student body. But for some students, their disability necessitates a different instructional method. This might include intensive phonemic awareness instruction, multi-sensory methods for comprehending new vocabulary, alternate math strategies or guided study skills.

The word "special" in SDI is a strong clue word. Special educators are able and obligated to bring a different perspective to designing and implementing instruction. With their pre-service training and in-service opportunities, job-embedded experiences and different mindsets, they can create adapted methods. I find it helpful to ask myself each day "What am I doing today that is special?" I encourage administrators to ask their special educators, whether in pull-out or inclusive settings, "What are you doing today that is special?" These questions will help to refocus special education teachers on their most important job responsibility.

3   To adapt delivery of instruction

The law does not give us any detail about the meaning of "adapt delivery," but it is clear that it should be different than the typical activity of a general education classroom. For example, an intensive use of small group instruction – more than typical – is likely to be adapted delivery. So, too, would be an intentional decrease in pacing. Computer-based learning programs may constitute adapted delivery, but only if they are different than what students without IEPs are using. Many experts consider co-teaching to be 'adapted delivery' and therefore qualify as SDI. However, this is only true if the co-teaching meets the standards set in the next section of the law.

Why Focus on SDI?

In addition to the three "whats" of SDI, the legislation includes the three "whys" or purposes of SDI.

1   To address the *unique needs* that result from the child's disability

A child's unique needs are often commensurate with an achievement gap. Team members write specific IEP goals to address these needs and gaps. The purpose of SDI, therefore, is to address these IEP goals with a frequency and intensity that will lead to meeting the goals in the time indicated. If a special education teacher is providing adaptations that address IEP goals, most likely they are providing specially designed instruction.

Students with disabilities also receive accommodations to help them accomplish their goals, but accommodations are *not* SDI. Yes, they are linked to IEP goals, but they are not instructional in nature. They are tools that may be available to all students in a classroom.

(See Chapter 6 for a more thorough exploration of the role of IEP goals.)

2   To *ensure access* of the child to the general curriculum

The purpose of SDI is to *ensure access* to the general curriculum, not just allow access. The word ensure is synonymous with words such as promise, guarantee and certify. SDI sets an expectation of empowerment for special educators. What will we do to make access a reality for all students? How will we make this promise come true? Inclusive settings make this reality more likely for the vast majority of our students. It is quite difficult to ensure access to the general curriculum if the student is being pulled out of the general education setting. While special education teachers are highly qualified in SDI, they may not be as qualified in the curriculum as their general education counterparts. In separate settings, students will not have exposure to the breadth and depth of discussion that peers without disabilities can bring to a topic. Precious minutes are lost as students are moved from place to place – time that they cannot afford to lose.

Special educator Johnny Cataffo once said, "You can't teach a child to swim by taking them out of the pool." I like to add "nor by just throwing them in!" This is where SDI is crucial – a life-saving intervention. Students who are included in general education settings, rather than pull-out, are more likely to have equitable access to the curriculum that the community has deemed critical for success.

3   So that the child can *meet* the educational standards that apply to all children.

The use of the word *meet* was very intentional. The goal of specially designed instruction is not just to move students forward, not just to expose them to the curriculum, but to *meet* the standards that apply to their non-disabled peers. What would special education look like if we truly adopted this goal? How might our practices change if we committed to high expectations and standards for all learners? The role of the special education teacher is to pledge their time and talents to adapting for and instructing each unique child so that they reach this goal. These efforts are what SDI is all about.

SDI in Context

A framework is a conceptual structure that guides us in building something useful. Frameworks have filled the educational horizon throughout history, sometimes yielding utility, sometimes yielding confusion. Several frameworks relate to specially designed instruction and may yield a bit of both.

Universal Design for Learning (UDL) is a framework first posed in the 1980s and developed extensively by the Center for Applied Special Technology (CAST). UDL calls educators to intentionally design education that is accessible to all by offering multiple means of engagement, representation and expression. Student voice and choice are strongly encouraged so that learners find relevance, become motivated and develop life-long learning skills. While UDL was originally meant as a means to address the needs of those with disabilities, it has evolved to being recognized as a framework that can help schools transform how to "advance the promise of effective instruction for every learner" (Ralabate and Berquist 2020, p. 5). The focus is on designing lessons and environments for a group of students, rather than for the individual, eliminating barriers in order to create access for all. UDL is *not* a special education strategy. Instead, accommodations and special education go above and beyond the UDL that is in place.

Differentiated Instruction (DI) is a framework, made most popular by Carol Ann Tomlinson, that suggests learning is most effective when teachers account for students' readiness levels, interests and learning preferences. Teachers respond to these differences by building variety into the content, process, product, and learning environment. Tomlinson explains, "teachers who differentiate provide specific alternatives for individuals to learn as deeply as possible and as quickly as possible, without assuming one student's road map for learning is identical to anyone else's" (2017, p. 4). DI is often viewed as a reactive process in which a teacher uses assessment information about each individual student to plan for how to effectively meet their needs. This view leads many teachers to feel that DI is an overwhelming amount of work. However, others consider DI to be a proactive process for lesson design, able to be structured in ways that are efficient and effective. DI is a general education practice that benefits all students, including those with disabilities, but is *not* SDI.

Multi-Tiered Systems of Support (MTSS) is defined in the federal Every Student Succeeds Act (2015) as "a comprehensive continuum of evidence-based, systemic practices to support a rapid response to students' needs, with regular observation to facilitate data-based instructional decision making." The law places responsibility on each state to adopt or develop a framework with multiple tiers of support and ensure implementation so that all students succeed. This means that there are different frameworks used under the MTSS label. Most MTSS frameworks include multiple gating procedures, functional assessments and flexibility in movement through the tiers so that students rapidly receive what they need. MTSS is a general education practice that students with disabilities benefit from.

Where does SDI fit within these related contexts? Table 3.1 shows a textual comparison while Figure 3.1 provides a visual representation. A student with an IEP still receives high-quality instruction, differentiation and supports, **as well as** specially designed instruction. As described in Chapter 1, some people can choose their own running shoes and master a 5k on their own but for others, supportive shoes and group encouragement, like MTSS and DI, are not enough. They also need individual assessment, short-term benchmarks and coaching that is tailored to their unique needs. With the entire package, they are ready to successfully reach their goal. Likewise, SDI is determined necessary by a team when a student with disabilities needs instruction that goes beyond what UDL, DI and MTSS bring to the classroom.

As you consider these frameworks, recognize that the terms UDL, DI and MTSS can all be interpreted and implemented in numerous ways. SDI differs in that it is a legally defined and federally mandated service, without being left up to individual states or districts. However, as you have seen, the law does not provide an abundance of detail and examples. Therefore, the responsibility lies on thoughtful educators to interpret SDI in ways which provide meaningful benefits for students with disabilities while being what the US Supreme Court calls "appropriately ambitious" (Endrews, 2016, p. 3).

An **accommodation** is a change in materials or procedures that enables students to participate in the curriculum and assessment in a way that allows their abilities and knowledge to be expressed and assessed. **Accommodations do not change what information is learned or measured** but are tools that enable a student to more readily access curricular content and to more easily demonstrate understanding of the content. Accommodations may be available to all students but may also be mandated through a 504 Plan or an IEP for a student with disabilities. Accommodations are not SDI.

A **modification** either directly or indirectly alters the curriculum and the assessment, resulting in **alternate standards** for a particular student as compared to grade level peers. Modifications should occur only for a small percentage of students for whom the team has decided to use alternate standards. These students typically have significant disabilities and IEP goals that reflect entry skills rather than grade level skills. SDI should always be present when a student is receiving modifications.

Examples and Non-Examples

Imagine reading a mystery novel in which you have been provided with characters, a setting, rising action, a climax and lots of clues, but no conclusion.

Table 3.1 Context for SDI

	UDL	DI	MTSS	SDI
Type	Conceptual Framework	Conceptual Framework	Conceptual Framework	Special Education Service
Legal authority	Considered best practice. Defined in federal law but not specifically required. Several states require evidence of UDL. Endorsed by CCSS and ESSA. See http:// www.cast.org/impact/ udl-public-policy	Considered best practice but not legally required or defined.	Legally required in some form in order for states to receive federal education funding through ESSA.	Legally required by IDEA for students with disabilities whose needs go beyond accommodations.
Process	Offering multiple means of engagement, representation and expression for all students. Embedded elements include ensuring accessibility & flexibility, offering choice and decreasing barriers to learning.	Addressing varied readiness levels, student interests and learning preferences through content, process, product and learning environment.	Providing increasingly intensive levels of intervention for students experiencing an academic, behavioral or social/emotional gap.	Adapting content, methodology or delivery of instruction to meet unique needs of a child with a disability.

(Continued)

Table 3.1 (Continued)

	UDL	DI	MTSS	SDI
Trigger	Proactive to needs/barriers within the lesson and learning environment, with a focus on the group.	Proactive and reactive to individual needs based on formative assessments.	Proactive and reactive to individual needs based on formative assessments.	Initially reactive to individual needs determined by a variety of formal evaluations and informal assessments to determine eligibility for special education. Special educators then become proactive in ongoing instructional planning.
Eligibility	Available to whole class, including students with IEPs.	Available to whole class, including students with IEPs.	Available to whole class, including students with IEPs.	Available only to individual students with IEPs.
Integration	UDL classrooms typically incorporate DI and MTSS and may include SDI for students with IEPs.	DI classrooms typically incorporate MTSS, may include UDL principles and may include SDI for students with IEPs.	MTSS typically incorporates DI and may take place within a UDL classroom. Students receiving SDI may be included in MTSS.	SDI goes beyond the practices found in UDL, DI and MTSS. SDI might occur in a classroom not incorporating UDL or DI.

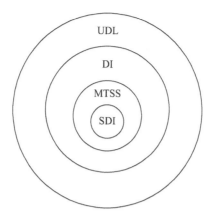

Figure 3.1 SDI in Context

Some readers will feel intrigued by the puzzle, while others may feel a bit frustrated. This is similar to the legislation written about SDI – the authors gave us some information but left us to determine other pieces on our own, using the clues they provided. The legislation does not offer any specific examples of SDI for us to learn from, compare to or ruminate on. Educators are left to puzzle it out, using clues, logic, experience and case law.

Consider five-year-old Bashir, with a goal on his Individualized Education Plan (IEP) that states:

> *Bashir will demonstrate skills for school success by following teacher's verbal directions (clean area, put personal items away, complete classroom routines).*

His special education teacher, Miss Linder, provides services in his kindergarten classroom three times per week. When she is present, she makes eye contact with Bashir before repeating the teacher's verbal directions. She models how to start the cleanup routine and verbally praises him when he begins. She circulates around the room, but checks in on Bashir more than other students.

Is this specially designed instruction? Let's look at some questions that can guide our decision-making process.

Guiding Questions for SDI

- ◆ Is it special? Something different from the typical general education practices of UDL or DI?
- ◆ Does it address the child's unique needs?
- ◆ Is it related to an IEP goal? Are we collecting data for progress monitoring?
- ◆ Is it instruction rather than a tool or accommodation?

- ◆ Is it intentional? Designed to bring about progress?
- ◆ Is it growing a skill that will be transferrable or generalizable?
- ◆ Is it building independence?

You may have answered "yes" to some questions and "no" to others. Yes, the special education teacher's efforts are linked to his unique needs and IEP goals, while addressing a skill that will lead to independence in other settings. No, it is not special. The classroom teacher most likely repeats her directions frequently to her young charges and models the necessary tasks. Is it intentional instruction, likely to bridge the gap between Bashir's current levels and the general expectations? Not as described here. In this scenario we see a special education teacher providing some on-the-spot minimal prompting. Unless Miss Linder adds a stronger instructional component to her interactions with him, she is doing what a general education teacher or paraeducator might do in the same circumstances.

Now consider a different experience for Bashir. Miss Linder arrives in the kindergarten a few minutes prior to classroom cleanup time. She quickly pulls Bashir and two of his peers to a small group as "special helpers." Miss Linder displays three photos of the cleanup process and asks the children to place them in the correct sequence as quickly as they can. She uses a pre-taught gesture for "listen" so that Bashir listens closely as she asks his peers to discuss how fast they should work. The three students choose a goal time for finishing the cleanup task and Bashir sets the time on Miss Linder's timer. She then turns the sequence pictures over and asks Bashir to recall the three steps in the cleanup sequence and say them aloud. When the classroom teacher gives the direction to cleanup, Bashir gets to work while Miss Linder observes him and collects behavioral data.

Is this specially designed instruction? Look back at the Guiding Questions for SDI to help you decide.

Our clues help us to examine the service Miss Linder is providing. Miss Linder has intentionally prepared instruction specific to Bashir's IEP goal and is collecting data on his progress. Repeated instruction and fading will eventually lead to independence and transfer. This level of direct instruction and intensity is typically not possible for a general education teacher with responsibilities for twenty to thirty students. It is special – an adaptation to the methodology used in the class. We can answer "yes" to each of the guiding questions, helping us to be confident that this is an example of SDI.

Layla is in Mrs. Montgomery's eighth-grade language arts class. Layla struggles with reading comprehension, as evidenced in a few of her IEP goals:

- ◆ Layla will draw inferences from text and link them to supporting text evidence.

- ◆ Layla will analyze a multi-page text to determine two main ideas.
- ◆ Layla will draw on specific details from a text to describe the setting or events.

Mrs. Montgomery meets weekly with the special education teacher, Mr. Perez, to co-plan the reading lessons. In the coming unit, there are several opportunities to work on main ideas and details. They identify a handful of students, including Layla, that would benefit from an adapted strategy for determining the difference. Mr. Perez suggests the Bull's Eye Strategy – one that has proved successful in the past. He sketches his idea out for Mrs. Montgomery to see (Figure 3.2).

He explains how students use sticky notes to capture ideas from the text, placing them on the dartboard based on their value or importance as a main idea. Mr. Perez points out that the center circle is only large enough for three sticky notes, so students will have to create questions to judge which ideas to move to a place of lesser importance in the outer circles. He will guide them in creating criteria or questions and give them several application opportunities with various brief texts. For each application exercise, he will take a photo of Layla's dartboard to see if she is improving her understanding of main

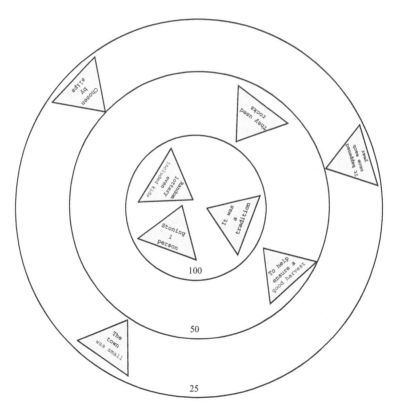

Figure 3.2 Bull's Eye

ideas versus details. Mrs. Montgomery suggests that about half the students in their class could benefit from this method and recommends that they split the class. She can teach an enrichment lesson for half the class, while Mr. Perez teaches the Dart Board Strategy to the other.

Is this specially designed instruction? Use the Guiding Questions for SDI to help you decide.

Mr. Perez's method is new to Mrs. Montgomery and based on what he believes will help Layla to make progress on her related IEP goals. By guiding students to develop criteria by which they can evaluate whether something is a main idea or a supporting detail, and adding a visual connection, he is instructing for independence and transfer. Layla's progress is monitored so that he can adapt again if necessary. Mr. Perez is providing specially designed instruction to Layla. But what about the other students? Is it still SDI if it is provided to a large group? The term SDI is a legal term that applies only to students receiving special education. The other students in the group are receiving high-yield instruction from Mr. Perez and incidental benefit from the skills he brings to the class.

On another day, Mr. Perez brings his tool bucket into the classroom. It is filled with highlighters, sticky arrows, scrap paper, erasers, fidget items and work masks. Today Mrs. Montgomery will be distributing a single-page article, dense with print and a complex graph. He is concerned that Layla and a few other students will find it difficult to stay focused and locate the details they need to participate in the class discussion. He gives each of these children two different-colored sticky arrows and a work mask into which they can slide their paper, as seen in Figure 3.3. As Mrs. Montgomery leads the lesson, Mr. Perez circulates, pausing as he passes these children to place their sticky arrow at the part of the text that is being discussed. He whispers words of encouragement in their ears.

Is this specially designed instruction? Use the Guiding Questions for SDI to help you decide.

"Is it instructional rather than a tool or accommodation?" This is the most important question to consider for this scenario. While many of the other questions might be answered "yes," this one is answered "no." Work masks and sticky arrows, while helpful, are not instruction. They can be extremely effective accommodations, along with things like highlighters, larger font, graphic organizers and extra time for testing. Special educators must prioritize their time and talents for adapting instruction rather than just making accommodations. If a student only needs accommodations, they do not become eligible for special education services, but are served instead by general education teachers. In this scenario, Mr. Perez is providing tools or accommodations, not instruction.

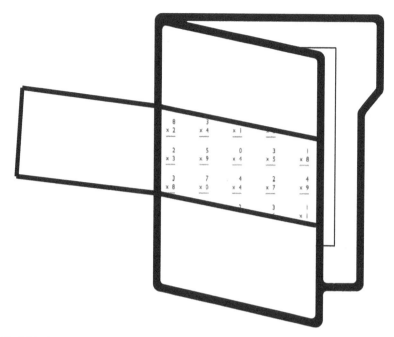

Figure 3.3 Work Mask

With this in mind, it becomes clear that the following examples would not qualify as SDI either. Instead, they are examples of tools or accommodations.

- Graphic organizers
- Extra white space on a test
- Preferential seating
- A printed version of the slides
- Partially completed notes
- An augmentative communication device
- Fidget items
- Highlighter tape
- Vocabulary flash cards
- An individual schedule
- Text or test read aloud
- Peer helper
- A word bank

Most great mysteries have several plot twists that encourage the reader to reconsider what they thought they knew. SDI also has twists that can cause quick conclusions to be turned upside down with new information.

Let's reconsider the first item in the previous list of accommodations – graphic organizers. These are highly effective, evidence-based tools that have become common in general education classrooms. They are also commonly found on IEPs under the accommodations listing. But there might be a circumstance in which graphic organizers become part of a specially designed lesson that fits the SDI criteria. Let's explore an example:

Jaxon struggles with organizing his thoughts, especially in his US Government class. Last year, his special education teacher added an IEP goal that reads:

> Jaxon will construct graphic organizers to assist in understanding and memorizing information from lectures and texts.

Mrs. Holt sees Jaxon once each week in her resource room to provide him with SDI related to study skills and self-advocacy. She creates a lesson for Jaxon that explores the various shapes and lines that are commonly used in graphic organizers. They discuss color and imagery, browsing through examples of sketch notes online. She guides Jaxon to create his own legend for the meaning of shapes, lines and colors so that he can use it in the future. Rather than simply providing him with a pre-formatted graphic organizer (an accommodation) she teaches him how to intentionally develop his own tools for maximum impact. In this way, the tool is part of the lesson but isn't the focus. *Instruction* is prioritized so that Jaxon receives the SDI promised to him. SDI can encompass accommodations as part of the instructional process, but is not simply an accommodation.

Like it or not, the authors of the legislation chose to leave the mystery incomplete. They did not specify a list of examples or non-examples of SDI for us. Instead, we must rely on those three powerful words, specially designed instruction, and the components of its definition, to tease out the answers for our students.

What Are the Benefits?

When we solve the puzzles built into a mystery novel, our brains release dopamine. Dopamine is most commonly known as a feel-good neurotransmitter, but it has additional benefits such as improved attention, motivation and memory. Similarly, it is commonly accepted that specially designed instruction helps students with disabilities learn, while also having additional benefits.

Support for Unidentified Students

Many a teacher has lost sleep over the students who fall through the cracks—those students who are not identified for special services or extra help but are struggling. When special educators collaborate with general educators, they can use their expertise to have an impact on learning for all students in a class, not just those with labels. The creative instructional adaptations that address a student's IEP goal may also be effective for others in a class. The general education teacher who is open to new ideas may begin to adopt some of the strategies and weave them into instruction throughout the day, year after year, impacting the lives of hundreds of other children.

Professional Growth

Searching. Reflecting. Hypothesizing. Creating. Evaluating. These are just some of the thought-provoking processes that educators go through when planning for and implementing SDI. Initially time-intensive, it becomes more efficient and fluid with practice. Teachers curate go-to resources recognize patterns that can be intentionally replicated and find a deep rhythm to their creative collaborations. The professional growth that occurs not only increases student success but increases teacher satisfaction and self-efficacy. In other words, SDI benefits the giver and the receiver. This benefit is magnified when teachers are working collaboratively to share expertise and design instruction through co-teaching and inclusive practices. The special educator improves their curriculum and content knowledge, the general educator gains instructional strategy expertise, and students reap the outcomes. A win-win-win!

Student Engagement

Several factors are related to high engagement. Robert Marzano and Debra Pickering, noted authors and researchers, identified the four major components of engagement as emotion, student interest, an understanding of importance, and a sense of efficacy (2010). SDI allows educators to consider all four of these when creating unique lessons for students with disabilities. This is especially crucial for students who have a history of school failure and have begun to disengage. As authors Washor and Majkowski remind us, students may "drop out in their heads—gradually disengaging from what schools have to offer" (2014). And we know that students with disabilities actually drop out of school at alarming rates—almost a third of students in the US public school system (https://nces.ed.gov/programs/digest/d18/tables/dt18_219.46.asp). SDI offers a process for overcoming the formidable forces of disengagement through individualization and efficacy-focused interventions.

High Expectations

"I didn't know she could do that!" Too often this exclamation is used by educators who hold low expectations for students with disabilities. Specialists and classroom teachers are frequently surprised by students who rise to the higher expectations of the general education curriculum. Researcher John Hattie's meta-analysis of teaching practices identified high expectations as one of the most impactful things teachers can do to bring about significant growth (2012). The legal definition of SDI requires us to keep our eye on this prize as we help students meet the standards. In 1984, special education researcher Anne Donnellan gave us a term for this—the least dangerous assumption. When we consider students with disabilities, we can assume competence or incompetence. It is less dangerous to assume competence in our students and be wrong than to assume incompetence and be wrong. Teachers who embrace a competence mindset will have the energy to sustain their own growth as well as their students.

Positive Behavior Support

Teachers frequently cite behavior problems as one of the biggest impediments to learning. While the root cause of behaviors varies tremendously, behavior is always communicative. It might communicate an emotional state, a desire for attention, frustration, boredom, or a myriad other messages. Some students with disabilities may have significant behavior disorders that are complex and difficult to interpret, with numerous related IEP goals. Other students with specific learning disabilities may display inappropriate behaviors only when faced with academic challenges. Patient, solution-oriented educators offer specially designed instruction so that students develop the skills, behaviors and attitude necessary to be successful in school and life beyond school. Functional behavioral assessments, explicit teaching of skills, and positive, goal-directed feedback are all considered high-leverage practices for students in special education (McLeskey et al. 2017).

Acceptance of Diversity

Take a look inside any school and you will see a kaleidoscope – students of different colors, sizes, talents – all blending together into one masterpiece of learning. Children who grow up in spaces where diversity is cherished are able to easily embrace diversity in the world around them. As global collaboration increases, graduates who are comfortable with diversity will be more successful. Sir Ken Robinson beautifully expressed this idea. "As humanity becomes more numerous and interwoven, living respectfully with diversity is not just an ethical choice, it is a practical imperative" (2015, p. 49). Gary Howard, an expert in culturally responsive practices, connects this benefit to social justice. "When we acknowledge who is caught in the achievement gap – the same racial, cultural, and economic groups that have been marginalized by the larger dynamics of dominance in our society – it becomes clear that 'education for all' and 'justice for all' are synonymous goals. The work of transforming public education in the service of equity, inclusion, and excellence for all of our children, is social justice work" (2007, p. 45). Specially designed instruction embraces diversity and spreads the message to those within reach. The student with an IEP feels validated as an individual, students around him are taught that we all have unique talents and struggles, and teachers walk the talk of social justice in meaningful ways.

To Sum Up

- ◆ SDI is a legal term that means to adapt content, methodology or delivery of instruction for students with disabilities. In essence, this is the role of a special education teacher.
- ◆ While the law does not provide a list of SDI examples, it provides us with clues so that we can reach thoughtful decisions about the effectiveness of our practices. When service is linked to IEP goals, includes specialized instruction, and leads to independence and transfer, it is likely to be SDI.
- ◆ The benefits of SDI include high expectations, student engagement and learning, increased acceptance of diversity and professional growth for educators.

Reflection Questions

- ◆ The law describes three purposes of SDI – 1) to address unique needs, 2) provide access to general education curriculum, 3) so that students will meet the standards. Why are all three of these purposes important?
- ◆ Think of a lesson you have witnessed, written or taught to a student with a disability. Was there an SDI element? UDL? DI? MTSS?
- ◆ How would you prioritize the benefits of SDI that were mentioned? Why?

Try This

- ◆ Survey two or more special educators to find out their understanding of the terms specially designed instruction, accommodations and modifications. What conclusions can you draw?
- ◆ Dig into school district documents to see what references there are to SDI. Notice where and how often it is mentioned. Based on your findings, consider advocacy steps you might take to improve the provision of SDI in the district.

4

Teaming for Student Success

The orchestra members file onto the stage and take their seats, arranging their tuxedo tails or gowns and adjusting their music stands. After a few moments, the first violinist plays a loud, clear note so that the musicians can check their tuning. A cacophony erupts until they find the sweet spot and are in sync. The conductor, patiently waiting backstage, emerges from behind the curtain to the excited applause of the audience. She shakes hands with the first violinist, a respectful tradition that honors the value of their collaboration. An anticipatory hush falls over the room, the baton is raised, and the symphony begins with a beautiful blending of instruments.

Early the next morning, the conductor reluctantly awakes to her alarm and hops out of bed to bang on the doors of her two children. "Time to get up for school!" She smells the coffee brewing – her husband's contribution to their morning routine – as she pulls on her robe and heads downstairs. Grabbing bread, cheese, veggies and fruit, she sets up an assembly line so that her children can make their school lunches. Next she puts bowls, spoons, cereal boxes and milk on the table, all while sidestepping her husband's attempts to pour them both coffee and fill juice glasses. A few minutes later, the children dressed, fed and carrying lunches in their school bags, they are out the door with dad for the ride to school.

Throughout the day, the conductor teams in several other ways. She plays doubles in tennis with friends, she participates in a virtual staff meeting to develop next season's program and she has an after-school conference with her daughter's teacher. At times she leads the team, while at others she is a follower.

Teaming abounds in most of our lives, even when we are not a musician, parent or athlete. Teaming has existed since the beginning of the human race, naturally evolving to help us survive. Our knowledge and research base about teaming also continues to evolve, bringing new insights that can dramatically improve our teaming practices.

> "Team" is a noun, a static term, that refers to a number of people with a common goal.
> "Teaming" is a verb that captures the activity of working together. It represents a living, changing process that individuals experience together.

Team Members

Like our conductor, educators participate in several different teams throughout the day, each with varying purposes, protocols and effectiveness. Teaming for specially designed instruction may include various blends of the following individuals:

Student

At the heart of the SDI process, the student with an IEP is an active participant in bringing about success. As you read this chapter, think about how you might be more intentional at engaging the student in the team. What information can they provide? What insights, preferences and perspectives do they bring?

Parent

As special education expert Mitchell Yell reminds us, "Certainly, parents have a unique and extremely important perspective on their child's strengths and needs. The combined knowledge and resources of parents and school district personnel help ensure that students have an opportunity to make progress" (2020, p. 345). Too often, parents, treasure troves of information, are given the opportunity for input only at the annual IEP meeting. How might we more frequently engage them in the SDI process, while still being efficient?

Special Education Teacher

Likened to the conductor or team captain, the primary responsibility for SDI lies with the special educator. Legal mandates place them at the center of the action, but so does their rich knowledge base and practical playbook. The special education teacher's competence and confidence levels must be high in order to help the team reach their goals. How might the special educator assertively lead the process while respecting others' contributions?

General Education Teacher

The primary purpose of SDI is to help students with unique needs access the same curriculum and meet the same standards as those of the general population. General education team members are the experts in curriculum and standards and understand what the minimum expectations should be at various grade levels. Students with disabilities should be thought of as general education students who receive the additional service of special education. Therefore, these teachers are integral to an SDI team. How can we capitalize on their expertise?

> Students with disabilities should be thought of as general education students who receive the additional service of special education.

Paraeducator

Also known as instructional assistants, teacher aides or paraprofessionals, these adults are vital to a team's success. Paraeducators often see students in a greater number of settings than any other team member – getting off the bus, in various classrooms, in the cafeteria, to name just a few. Information they gather from these environments and experiences will deepen our understanding of student strengths and needs. In addition, the level of fidelity with which they implement team decisions will be key to successful generalization. When and how can we communicate with them most effectively about SDI?

English Language Development Specialist

In today's classrooms, many students are learning English as a second or third language. Whether they have disabilities or not, the ELD specialist plays an important part on the team. Using their training and skills, they can help to assess how much of the student's struggle is due to language vs. something else. They can transform lessons by adding scaffolds for language and instructional strategies that yield benefits to more than just English Language Learners.

Related Professional

Students with disabilities may receive services from a speech/language pathologist, mobility specialist, occupational therapist, school psychologist and more. Each of these professionals brings a very specific area of expertise that may cross over into all areas of instruction. Transdisciplinary teaming requires a greater level of communication among disciplines, resulting in better services for students. What cross-overs might we want to build upon so that the student receives more unified services?

Interventionist

This broad term might include educators who focus on Tier 2 and 3 services for students, those who have an expertise in literacy or math, or anyone whose responsibility is to add intervention support for students who are struggling. How might we find out what skills and talents they bring to the team so that they can be fully utilized?

Instructional Coach

This relatively new position defies easy description, as each school or district defines it differently. Typically, an instructional coach operates in the land between teaching and supervision, helping interested teachers to map out their learning journey and then offering to walk alongside them. During the SDI process, an instructional coach might be invited to observe, facilitate, provide feedback or even model a skill. A wise team utilizes any assets a building staff has to offer. At what points in the SDI process will an instructional coach add the most value?

School Administrator

As discussed in Chapter 12, school leaders and administrators can support SDI in many ways. Perhaps most importantly, leaders can clarify the "why" with an inclusive vision of students with disabilities as capable and equal members of the school community. Administrators can also help clarify roles and resources, so that teams know what is available and what is expected. How might the administrator present themselves as a member of the team, ready and willing to support SDI?

Individual Contributions

Each team will be composed differently, with shifting membership throughout a student's school career. While the popular saying, "There is no I in team," is literally true, it can lead to faulty thinking. Teams are made up of individuals with different backgrounds, needs and motivations. Individual members also have different skills in teaming, from highly effective at teaming to what many might call 'not a team player.' Any individual can have a significant impact on team success, especially within teams that work together over a long time (Bender et al. 2012). A *Teaming "I" Quotient* reflects an individual's contribution to the active, effective process of teaming. Use the following self-assessment to determine your score and reflect on how you collaborate (Table 4.1).

Table 4.1 Teaming "I" Quotient

Directions: Choose a specific team to consider. Give yourself points for each statement as it applies to your participation on that team.

0=Never 1=Rarely 2=Occasionally 3=Usually 4=Always

"I" Statements	Points
1 I am aware of our team purpose.	
2 I ensure that team members know our purpose.	
3 I assist in clarifying our purpose when needed.	
4 I believe we have a goal that is attainable.	
5 I care about achieving our team goal(s).	
6 I contribute toward achieving our goal(s).	
7 I seek diversity of knowledge and talent contributions from team members.	
8 I seek diversity of perspectives from team members.	
9 I seek out resources that we need for better teaming.	
10 I actively listen to others and ask questions of the team.	
11 I attend to the non-verbal cues of my teammates.	
12 I notice when there is an imbalance in conversational turn-taking.	
13 I encourage all to speak so that we have balanced input.	
14 I avoid making rude or negative comments about others.	
15 I share authentic experiences that may make me vulnerable.	
16 I show respect to my team members.	
17 I allow myself to take risks when problem solving.	
18 I engage in courageous conversations when I have a difference with a team member.	
19 I persevere through difficulty.	
20 I follow the team-developed norms.	
21 I know my teammates' communication preferences.	
22 I follow through with tasks or commitments so that team members can depend on me.	
23 I celebrate progress with my team members.	
24 I share credit and blame (we vs. me).	
25 I participate in professional learning opportunities so that I can better help the team accomplish our goal(s).	
TOTAL "I" QUOTIENT	/100

Effective Teaming

What Works

Many of us are familiar with a teaming framework posed by psychologist Bruce Tuckman in the 1960s. Tuckman suggested that all teams go through four stages of development. Borrowing from the field of poetry, Tuckman named these stages Forming, Storming, Norming, and Performing. Forming is characterized by polite, tentative behavior. Partners are feeling each other out, usually being on their best behavior. Storming, Tuckman's second stage, is when partners start to be more honest about their differences. Disagreements arise and are handled with professionalism (hopefully!). As teams do this, they develop norms for working together and eventually perform in an effective manner. Tuckman's framework has been applied to teaming, in almost every discipline, for more than a half-century. But what current data do we have that might inform our teaming in evidence-based ways?

In 2012, Google embarked on a multi-year quest, code-named Project Aristotle, to determine what makes teams more or less effective (Duhigg 2016). At first, patterns were hard to see. Some successful teams were made up of friends, while others were almost strangers. Some teams used a hierarchical structure while others were more democratic. Finally, a common feature appeared – successful teams had a specific set of group norms. Which norms? Earlier researchers had shown that the wrong norms can hobble a group (Wooley et al. 2010). Google's research found that the best teams have two characteristics or norms in common. First, all members speak in nearly the same proportion. When one dominates, the collective intelligence declines. This conversational balance may not happen in every short meeting but does occur over time. Second, team success is highly dependent on social sensitivity – the awareness of how teammates are feeling. People who actively attend to body language and tone of voice are more likely to respond with empathy and kindness. Empathy and vulnerability release oxytocin, the hormone associated with bonding and trust. These in turn lead to effective teaming and problem solving. Sociologist Brené Brown claims, "If you're not willing to build a vulnerable culture, you can't create." SDI team members may often feel vulnerable as they tackle the unusual challenges that students with disabilities can present. In order to enhance the ability to create solutions, time spent developing equity and social sensitivity norms will be time well spent.

Britt Andreatta, an award-winning thought leader, integrates her expertise in neuroscience and learning to offer a new vision of teaming that can also be applied to our goal of effective SDI (2018). After immersing herself in brain research, Andreatta developed a framework that accounts for when and why the human brain emits neurotransmitters like serotonin, oxytocin and cortisol – all crucial for teaming.

Picture four gates that teams must open and go through on their journey. Each gate represents potential for peak performance, depending on each individual team member.

Gate 1: Safety

Because safety is at the very core of our survival, we are very sensitive to threat. This includes worry about our livelihood and job security, but also rejection of ourselves or our contributions. When we first gather with a group, we scan and decide whether we feel safe or need to be wary. Negative initial impressions during this forming stage can be difficult to overcome. All team members must be conscious, especially in the early stages of this journey, of using behaviors that are respectful and socially sensitive.

Successful SDI requires creativity and out-of-the box thinking. Adapting content, delivery or methodology of instruction involves diverging from the typical path and developing ideas that address unique needs of a student with a disability. Teams that are open to unconventional thinking, willing to accept ideas without being harshly judgmental and encourage everyone to contribute are more likely to find solutions for their students. Balanced input, or "teamclusion," is an essential element of a strong team.

"Teamclusion" n. the act of valuing all members' participation in the work of the group

---

Gate 1 Action Steps

- ◆ Spend a few minutes upfront getting to know your teammates beyond their names and titles. Do they have an unusual talent or area of interest? Do they consider themselves an introvert or extrovert? How do they prefer to process information? Do they have any pet peeves you should know about? Asking these questions not only gathers pertinent information – it also demonstrates an interest in others and an openness to diversity.
- ◆ Discuss and decide upon a problem-solving process for the team. (This is not the same as how to design SDI. Instead, this is a process for discussing obstacles to effective teaming.) Many problem-solving models exist, but most include a few basic steps, represented in Figure 4.1. The Collaborative Solutions Worksheet. Notice that while

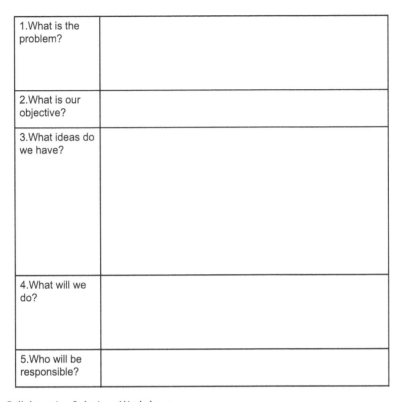

1.What is the problem?	
2.What is our objective?	
3.What ideas do we have?	
4.What will we do?	
5.Who will be responsible?	

Figure 4.1 Collaborative Solutions Worksheet

a large block of space is allocated to describing the problem, it is not unlimited. Teams that get stuck in this first step are spinning their wheels. Teams then agree on a unified objective that will address the main problem. The largest space on the worksheet is reserved for idea generation. This signifies that all ideas are welcomed, all voices heard. Only after idea generation is exhausted does the team create their action plan.

Gate 2: Purpose

A team's second gate is clarity of purpose. An individual working alone may have a very clear sense of their purpose, but teaming complicates things. Team members may have different intentions, reasons for or understandings of the what and why of the work. Not only does purpose guide our actions, but it also increases a feeling of psychological well-being and engagement. In this way it can build energy and boost us forward toward accomplishing our goal.

Two distinct challenges exist at this gate for SDI teams. The first challenge is to ensure that everyone understands the meaning of SDI and how it is different from general instruction or accommodations (see Chapter 2). A history of misunderstanding, or in some cases a total lack of understanding, is likely to have impacted the school culture regarding special education. Many staff members will have adopted beliefs and attitudes that may be contrary to the purpose of SDI. Teams will benefit from assessing members' understanding of SDI and adding clarity when necessary. The second challenge related to purpose is to ensure that each individual team member understands their role in SDI and what is expected of them. A move to more inclusive practices means that roles have changed for all involved. It is critical to define the new role with as much clarity as possible, while maintaining the flexibility needed for an ever-changing human endeavor. In addition, schools will need to consider legal requirements, teacher licensing and local bargaining agreements.

Gate 2 Action Steps

- Share the definition of SDI with all team members. Pose various student interventions and discuss whether they are examples or non-examples of SDI. Ask team members to explain their thinking until you reach consensus and are confident that the answer is in keeping with the legal requirements.
- Engage in the process of role clarification using the SDI Roles and Responsibilities Checklist Table 4.2 (Beninghof 2020). Be sure to avoid making assumptions about the assignment of responsibilities. Although some guidance can be mined from federal and state law, responsibility for many of the day-to-day tasks is left to each unique team to determine.

Gate 3: Belonging

Building on the work done to pass through the first two gates, this part of the journey is about developing a deep sense of trust and belonging. No longer in the forming stages, teams are now actively engaged in the work. Members need to feel that risk-taking and honest discussions are not only safe but encouraged. As Andreatta shares, "This acts as a boost because it frees up energy that was previously being used to maintain an 'appropriate' or 'professional' image. That's not to say that people become unprofessional but rather they are more authentic and vulnerable with each other." Team members feel a rhythm developing, with all players in sync, yet still adding

Table 4.2 SDI Roles and Responsibilities Checklist

Who Will Be Responsible For:	Name	Name	Name	Comments
Identifying places in the general education curriculum that link to IEP goals?				
Choosing the IEP goal(s) to be addressed during a lesson?				
Knowing the specific IEP goal(s) for the day?				
Designing the specially designed instruction that will occur?				
Selecting and organizing instructional materials?				
Introducing the specially designed instruction to the student?				
Continuing to implement the specially designed instruction?				
Collecting progress monitoring data?				
Planning for generalization to other conditions?				
Designing practice opportunities such as quizzes and homework?				
Scheduling students and staff so that SDI can occur?				
Providing any necessary training related to the SDI?				
Coordinating or directing team members (para-educators, related professionals, etc.)?				
Maintaining home contact related to SDI?				

their own unique sounds. Artistic director and jazz musician Wynton Marsalis described the artistic teaming he found at the Lincoln Center. "There are always tensions that come up. Part of working is dealing with tensions. If there's no tension, then you are not serious about what you're doing. But there's a certain warmth in there, too, and a familiarity."

Tensions may also arise when team members are working to implement SDI. A sense of belonging may feel fleeting as members leave the collaborative planning session to return to more isolated spaces. Teams will want to intentionally build mechanisms for checking in with each other, for celebrating student progress or collaboratively problem solving when plans aren't achieving the desired result. Susan Scott, author of *Fierce Conversations*, reminds us "No plan survives its collision with reality." SDI teammates that support each other during this collision will be able to maintain and even grow its collective energy level for the work still ahead.

Gate 3 Action Steps

◆ Develop an easily-accessible online community for your team. Begin by identifying the needs that can be addressed this way, such as last-minute changes to lesson plans, a research article for everyone to read, a copy of a recent Collaborative Solutions Worksheet or step-by-step directions for operating a student's new communication device. Then choose a system that is easy to maneuver (for any team members who are less proficient with technology) and shareable. Caution: remember at all times to follow legal and local guidelines regarding student privacy.

◆ Digital communication, while efficient, is not always effective and can sometimes even be confusing. Create a set of norms regarding your digital communications. When will you use email vs. text messages? How much response time is acceptable for each method? One creative team developed a shorthand to indicate the response time expected, i.e. 4H or 2D, adding excellent clarity to their digital communication norms. Be sure to also create in-person communication opportunities whenever possible.

Gate 4: Peak Performance

A team at this gate is so effective it becomes a game changer. A sense of psychological safety abounds, individuals take risks because they trust and respect one another, and they fully utilize the talents and strengths of each team member. They still encounter challenges – no teaming is free of obstacles – but they have the skills and commitment to grapple with them.

The process of specially designed instruction is often filled with plans that go awry, unexpected student responses, changes to physical environments and schedules and competing needs. Any one of these obstacles can be overwhelming for one individual. However, when effective teaming occurs, many carry the load. Perhaps the most striking examples of this are the inspirational videos of runners carrying injured runners across the finish line. Just as these athletes are committed to everyone accomplishing their goals, SDI team members are committed to doing whatever it takes, together, so that students are successful.

Gate 4 Action Steps

- Proactively create back-up plans for situations that might otherwise spin out of control. A good example of this falls within the realm of behavior plans. One school found that a special education co-teacher was often being called out of her co-taught class to respond to a student's outburst in another room. Not only was this disruptive to the students in the co-taught class; it was also dramatically impacting the teacher's dependability factor. The team came together and created a hierarchy of student behaviors (Level 1 to 5), listing the names of building staff that should be called at each level. This helped them all to realize that several people, not just the special education teacher, could interact with the student so that the co-teaching would not be continually disrupted.
- Celebrate successes, even the small steps forward. Mandy Leensvaart, an expert in school leadership, described her experience at celebrating student progress data. "For teachers to see the quantitative data only motivated additional work and dedication. Teachers get excited! They feel that what they are doing is making a difference." Find time to share your progress with all members of the team. Paraeducators are not always included in meetings where student progress is discussed. Be sure to include them in the celebration. Related professionals, usually itinerant, may be rushing in and out of the building. Find ways to include them in the celebration. Seeing progress increases perseverance with the task!

Team Problem Solving

Mrs. Toomey, a veteran speech/language pathologist, has been serving elementary students for many years. This year she joined an eighth-grade middle school team to co-teach language arts for the first time. Her co-teacher, Mrs. Carr, is recognized as one of the best in the district and usually teaches the advanced classes. Working with students with disabilities is a new challenge for her.

Before the school year started, they met to discuss roles and responsibilities, planning and teaching norms and grading practices. They also went out for lunch one day to get to know each other outside of their school personas. Their first few weeks of teaming went smoothly, with both partners taking the time to listen, understand and encourage the other. Halfway through the first marking period the honeymoon was over. Tensions rose and disagreements ended unresolved.

MRS. TOOMEY: I'm concerned that you aren't giving students enough time to talk about their ideas before they begin writing.

MRS. CARR: We don't really have time for that if we want to keep up with the pacing guide.

MRS. TOOMEY: Students with language disabilities really need to talk things out before putting them on paper. You won't get the results you want if you don't let them do this.

MRS. CARR: Whenever we let them talk, they usually go off-topic anyway. If it's an issue for one or two students, then maybe you can pull them off to the side and work with them.

MRS. TOOMEY: But that will just isolate them and shut them down even more. They've got to talk to their peers.

MRS. CARR: I don't know what you mean, "shut them down," but we just don't have any spare time in this writing unit.

What is causing the most difficulty for this team? What could Mrs. Toomey and Mrs. Carr do differently? What connections can you make between this scenario and your own collaborative teaming?

Now picture a different exchange.

MRS. TOOMEY: Our data shows that several students aren't adding much detail to their writing. This is especially true for our two with IEP goals in writing.

MRS. CARR: Well, the rubric for this unit's assessment has a strong emphasis on details. I just don't know how to find the time to change our approach without sacrificing something else.

MRS. TOOMEY: So, we agree that we need to emphasize details? And we might need to let go of one of our planned activities to find the time.

MRS. CARR: I'm feeling a bit overwhelmed at the moment – not sure how to do this.

MRS. TOOMEY: It can be overwhelming to fit in all the lessons and adapt for students with individual goals. I have an idea for how we could structure some peer-to-peer talk about details.

MRS. CARR: How long would that take?

MRS. TOOMEY: We can be flexible with it. I know that sometimes, as a speech/language specialist, I let them go on too long with their conversations. How much time do we think we can devote to this?

In this second telling of problem solving between Mrs. Carr and Mrs. Toomey, we see the partners clarifying the objective, sharing vulnerabilities, empathizing, asking questions, and using "we" language as they begin to solve their dilemma.

Relationships become more complicated when a hierarchical structure is in play. This is especially true for the interaction between a special education teacher and a paraeducator. The legal requirements, licensing and job descriptions make certain things clear and other things a bit cloudy.

Mr. Jackson is entering his third year as a high school special education teacher, with an affinity for working with students who exhibit challenging behaviors. Abdul, one of the students on his caseload, has been assigned a full-time paraeducator, Mrs. Sabbagh. She is a dedicated and valued team member, has been with the district for twenty years and is old enough to be Mr. Jackson's mother.

Abdul's behaviors began to change significantly a few months ago. Assessment revealed some shifting family dynamics, increased anxiety and anger and a desire for more attention at school. Abdul had found that inappropriate classroom behaviors such as calling out, cursing and getting out of his seat gained him lots of attention. These behaviors were escalating rapidly, so the team created a new behavior plan for him. The plan included instruction from Mr. Jackson to help Abdul self-advocate for his needs, as well as instruction from the school counselor on anger management strategies. All team members were expected to proactively provide specific praise and attention for appropriate behavior while ignoring the rest.

Right away, Mr. Jackson noticed that Mrs. Sabbagh was having a difficult time maintaining fidelity to the behavior plan. When Abdul called out, she would quietly say "shhh." When he would curse, she would remind him "watch your language." Her intentions were good, but her responses were undermining the plan. Mr. Jackson gently reminded her of their agreement to ignore inappropriate behavior, but these old habits were hard to break. He didn't want to cause a rift with Mrs. Sabbagh by continually reminding her.

What should Mr. Jackson do next? Where does his "I" Quotient fall short? What if Mrs. Sabbagh was a general education co-teacher instead of a paraeducator?

Students like Abdul need our SDI efforts to be consistent and relentless. For the sake of our students, we must be willing to engage in courageous conversations with teammates. Many teachers are reluctant to enter into difficult conversations. At my workshops, it is common for educators to share with me their frustration about their partnerships. When I ask whether they have talked honestly with their partners about the issue, the response is usually "no." Conflict Avoidance Syndrome (CAS), a devastating but curable condition, is rampant in most schools. People with CAS ignore symptoms, pretend everything is alright and refuse to swallow the difficult truth – that when we avoid uncomfortable conversations, it is our students that pay the ultimate price.

> **For the sake of our students, we must be willing to engage in courageous conversations with teammates.**

Civil rights activist Mary McLeod Bethune reminded us, "The progress of the world will call for the best that all of us have to give." At times, our best will be exciting and energizing, while at others it may require difficult conversations. When those best efforts are combined into a well-functioning team, wonderful things will happen for our students.

To Sum Up

◆ SDI teams can include a wide variety of people who each bring different personalities, experiences, perspectives and skills.

◆ Teaming is an active process that is impacted by each individual team member.

◆ Most teams proceed through stages or gates as they develop. Teams that are most effective at this have a high level of social sensitivity, actively ensure that input is balanced, and engage in courageous conversations.

Reflection Questions

◆ Do all members of the SDI team feel included? What have you done to include or exclude members?

◆ What role confusion might currently exist on your team? What makes you think so? What might you do to ameliorate the confusion?

Try This

- ◆ Review your "I" Quotient self-assessment and choose one area where you could improve. Develop an action plan with at least two steps you will undertake.
- ◆ Share the Four Gates framework with your teammates. Ask them where they see strengths and weaknesses. Discuss how the group might improve its teaming.

Part II
Planning for SDI

The process of "design thinking" was first published in 1965 by L. Bruce Archer, a professor at the Royal College of Art. Archer recognized that architects, engineers and other designers have a solution-centered focus, and work through several iterations as they create, test and recreate ideas. Design thinking often includes multiple opportunities for brainstorming and other creative exercises, especially those that help problem solvers take on the perspective of their stakeholders or customers. Specially designed instruction (SDI) not only provides us with the opportunity to do this, but also gives us the responsibility to do so.

Perhaps one of the authors of our legislation had heard of Archer's term and recognized the power of the word "design." By inserting it between "specially" and "instruction," they elevated the SDI process to include proactive analysis, evaluation and creativity. It is the rare educator who can offer effective SDI on the fly, without forethought or planning. For the rest of us, a structured planning process can guide us to create lessons that fruitfully incorporate SDI. The following seven step planning process will be explained in greater detail in the chapters of this part. Planning is followed by implementation and assessment so that we learn what works best for our students and can improve our next round of instructional design (Figure P2.1).

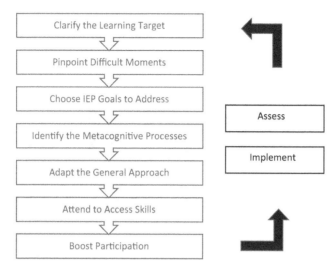

Figure P2.1 Planning Steps

Steps for Planning SDI

1   *Clarify the learning target for the lesson.*
     What do we want students to be able to know or do by the end of the period? Is the verb in the learning target flexible or constrictive? Does the verb represent lower-level or higher-level thinking?

2   *Pinpoint the difficult moments students may experience.*
     What has been a challenge in the past? What do we expect to be challenging, based on data and our knowledge of student capacities right now? Why is this difficult?

3   *Choose IEP goals to address during the lesson or lesson series.*
     Which goals are most closely aligned with the curriculum? Are there other goals, i.e. behavioral or communication, that could be addressed? Are there any students with similar goals?

4   *Identify the metacognitive process that a successful learner might use.*
     How does a successful learner think about this? Is there a strategy that I use, other than the one typically taught? How might I make this process tangible?

5   *Adapt the general approach.*
     How might we incorporate pre-teaching, visual and kinesthetic input, small-group instruction, explicit directions, chunking and other alternative methods? Is there a specific approach that will yield better skill generalization? Shall we transform the lesson for all or just a few?

6   *Attend to necessary access or executive function skills.*
    What learning behaviors will help the students be successful? Are
    there opportunities to address any executive function gaps? What
    can be put in place that yields greater independence?

7   *Build in specific methods to boost participation.*
    Why might a student not participate? What strategies or tools
    will lead to successful participation and engagement? What small
    grouping configurations will work best?

5

Planning Step 1:
Clarifying the Learning Target

The Appalachian Trail, affectionately known as the AT, is a public footpath that runs from Springer Mountain, Georgia to Mt. Katahdin, Maine, covering a distance of over 2100 miles. While it is currently well-maintained by the National Park Service, as well as several hiking clubs and volunteers, that was not always the case.

In 1955, Emma Gatewood set out to hike the entire distance with only a fourteen-pound sack of supplies slung over her shoulder, wearing sneakers. At the time, most people had never heard of the Appalachian Trail, nor were they interested in traversing its wild, isolated path. Detailed maps did not exist, shelters were few and far between and white blazes on the trees that served as trail markers were inconsistently maintained. But Emma Gatewood was determined. At 67 years old, "Grandma Gatewood," as she would become famously known, started her journey in Georgia in the spring, with the hope of making it to Maine before snow hit the mountains. While bad weather and fallen trees often caused her to divert from the trail, she was most frustrated by the times she became lost because of a lack of signs. For hikers, the painted blazes on trees are often the only solid evidence that you are on the right path. Unfortunately, these blazes were often worn away or missing all together, leaving Grandma Gatewood to hike unnecessary miles, retrace steps and extend her already arduous journey.

Fortunately, Gatewood drew attention to this national treasure and renewed interest in its upkeep. Thanks to her, day-hikers and thru-hikers can now wander into the woods and find their way back out safely without getting lost. Maps, trail signage and tree blazes guide ramblers and trekkers from the macro to the micro view so that they can experience the mountain vistas and return home to see their loved ones.

Whether you hike the local trails, take a road trip, or visit unknown cities, identifying your destination spot and the short-term markers along the way is smart planning. Without them, you are likely to get lost, experience frustration and take much longer to get to your destination. Worse yet, you may never get there at all! Learning targets are the destination markers that guide teachers and students on their learning journey. Clarity is a critical first step (Figure 5.1).

> Learning targets are the destination markers that guide teachers and students on their learning journey.

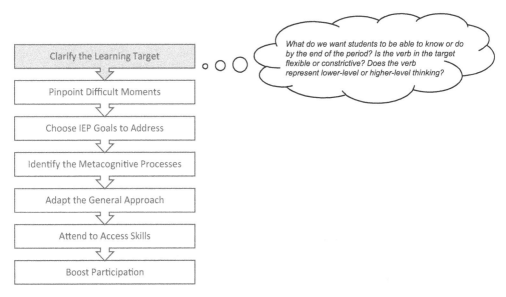

Figure 5.1 Planning Step 1

What Are Learning Targets?

Connie Moss and Susan Brookhart, university professors with wide-ranging educational backgrounds, tell us that learning targets guide learning by "describing, in language that students understand, the lesson-sized chunk of information, skills, and reasoning processes that students will come to know deeply" (2012, p. 3). When shared in comprehensible ways, students can see the lesson destination clearly and channel their efforts to staying on the trail. Instructional objectives and standards, on the other hand, are meant to guide teachers in their larger and longer-term quest. While derived from these bigger statements, learning targets help students to be present in the moment. Students can answer the question, "What will we accomplish today?"

Moore, Garst and Marzano (2018) pose that learning targets fall into three categories – *foundational, learning goal*, and *cognitively complex. Foundational* targets reflect the missing skills, lack of prior knowledge or incomplete processes that may interfere with success. Students with disabilities, those learning English, students with spotty attendance – all may need intentional work on foundational targets. *Learning goal* targets usually represent the grade-level expectation for the curricula. Finally, most classes will also have students who are ready for *cognitively complex* targets. Offering them rich, deep thinking that extend their experiences will keep them from boredom and disengagement. And just to keep us on our toes during this journey, we may have students in need of both foundational and complex targets! Teachers will need to plan for multiple levels, while not overwhelming students with too many learning targets. One or two will bring about focus, three or more will blur their view.

Benefits of Learning Targets

When learning targets are clearly written, effectively shared and used to guide instruction, benefits are bountiful. Positive outcomes occur for students, teachers and school leaders, as they all work together with clarity of purpose in actionable chunks. Child development research shows that learning targets help children improve their ability to self-regulate, monitor their progress and redirect their efforts to the task (Berk, 2003). Actionable chunks also allow students to see micro-progress, rather than waiting for a test or essay grade at the end of the week. Neurologist and teacher Judy Willis explains that achieving even a small goal releases dopamine. This neurotransmitter doesn't just make us feel good – it "boosts memory, attention span, ability to sustain effort, perseverance and motivation" (2015). Successful adults across all career paths have recognized the power of micro goals. Sabina Nawaz, a CEO coach for Fortune 500 companies, shares, "Big goals are more burdensome than they are motivational; they require daunting effort to accomplish and sustain in our busy lives. Falling short of a lofty goal creates a negative spiral of discouragement deterring future action." Instead, Nawaz recommends identifying a "ridiculously small" step.

From CEOs to kindergarteners, learning targets work. Heidi Heath DeStefano conducted action research with her kindergarten students, introducing learning targets to her intervention groups. She enthusiastically shares "Within the first week of implementation, it appeared that the learning targets would be highly effective. I felt rising elation as I saw the children becoming more enthusiastic and motivated as they took ownership of their learning. Assessment scores also steadily improved" (2019, p. 75).

Effective Learning Targets

Imagine a teacher at the beginning of a unit on essay writing. The instructional objective is to teach students how to choose from various planning formats. Consider two different ways that a teacher might start the first lesson. Which one has a clear, actionable learning target?

1 "Scholars, we are going to write three-paragraph essays this week. There are lots of steps in the process, but today we will be planning. You will be able to pick your own topic, so think of something you are interested in and know a lot about so that you can add details to your paragraphs. We will want lots of sensory details. Turn to a peer and share what topic you might like to write about. Yaslene, please repeat the directions out loud for everyone."

2 "Scholars, this week we will be learning how to plan, draft and revise a three-paragraph essay. By the end of today's class, you will be able to say, 'I can evaluate and choose a planning format.' You will explore a few different ways to plan, choose one that you think will work best for you and then create your plan. Let's read our learning target aloud together. *I can evaluate and choose a planning format*. Great. We will then get started creating our plans."

The first example provides the same big picture as the second, but has students thinking about their topic, rather than the planning process. If the teacher's instructional goal was to help students learn how to generate or choose a topic, then she might share a learning target such as "I can generate ideas and choose a topic for my writing." Instruction would then be focused on that skill. Students might also be thinking about details, something the teacher mentions twice. Again, if that is the instructional goal, then the learning target might be "I can generate four sensory details related to my topic" and the instruction would focus on how to reflect on the senses to add specific details.

The second example relates to the essay planning objective and provides clarity to the students so they can measure their success. While they will obviously still need a topic and details, the focus is on evaluating a variety of planning formats (i.e. outline, web, storyboard) and beginning to create the plan. When the teacher does a mid-lesson check-in, students will be able to measure their progress against the learning target. Were they able to evaluate the options? Did they make a choice they can justify? If not, they can adjust their learning behaviors, knowing exactly where they are supposed to be by the end of the lesson. In the last moments, they can return to the "I can..." statement and reflect on whether they accomplished it.

Effective learning targets have three characteristics:

1 They are written for one specific lesson.
2 They are written in student-friendly language.
3 They are focused on the learning, not the delivery method.

Using these characteristics, evaluate the following examples and highlight those that are well-written.

1 I can compare and contrast two non-fiction articles.
2 I can complete ten math stories on my worksheet.
3 I can describe the seven roles of the president of the US.
4 I can play Pass the Plate to generate synonyms.
5 I can collect observational data and input it into a data table.
6 I can produce a personal narrative.
7 I can infer a character trait from a descriptive text.
8 I can write all of the upper- and lowercase letters.
9 I can apply six different annotation marks while reading an expository article.
10 I can create a clay map showing the political boundaries of Europe in 1942.

Educators can readily have different opinions about the best wording of a learning target, based on current functioning levels of their students, national or regional standards, professional development experiences and personal preferences. With this in mind, the odd-numbered targets in the list above are the most well-written. They clarify the learning expectation for just one lesson without confusing the delivery method or activity with the learning.

Upping Your Game

For those ready to go beyond the basic characteristics of a learning target, you can up your game by carefully considering the verb. Is the verb flexible or constrictive? Patti Ralabate, an expert on Universal Design for Learning, encourages us to use flexible verbs so that the target is accessible to all. Constrictive verbs may limit students with specific disabilities. For example, a learning target that requires a student to compute is more flexible and accessible that one that requires adding or subtracting. See Table 5.1 for additional examples.

Special education teachers will also want to consider the rigor within their verb of choice. During my professional learning workshops, I often ask participants to compose learning targets of their choice on whiteboards around the room. As I circulate, I usually notice that the special educators tend to use lower-level thinking verbs like *identify, label* or *define* and rarely use verbs such as *analyze, evaluate* and *synthesize*. While some of our students will need these foundational targets, we must safeguard against skew toward assuming incompetence.

Table 5.1 Flexible and Constrictive Verbs

Examples of Flexible Verbs	Examples of Constrictive Verbs
• Produce	• Write
• Show	• Draw
• Compute	• Add/Subtract
• Share	• State
• Communicate	• Pronounce
• Select	• Outline
• Judge	• Diagram

Clarity for Team Members

Clarity of learning targets becomes even more critical when co-planning or co-implementing with others. If various team members interpret a learning target differently, instruction may go in several directions, leaving students confused, frustrated and disengaged.

Learning Targets in Action

Ms. Kyle, a special education teacher, received a text message from Mr. Foo, her chemistry co-teacher.

For Tuesday, our learning target is "I can use safety equipment during our lab work." Can you think of some lesson ideas about this before we meet?

Ms. Kyle ponders the target to make sure she understands it. She rightly figures that if she isn't sure exactly what it means, that several students in the class won't either. She can think of three teens that will follow the lead of their peers and simply use whatever they see others using. But does this mean they have achieved the learning target? What have they learned? She wonders if the target might be revised to state *"I can analyze the lab assignment and determine which safety equipment is necessary."*

As Ms. Kyle and Mr. Foo meet, Ms. Kyle shares her thoughts about the learning target. They discuss what the main emphasis should be – safe use or analysis. Mr. Foo, highly qualified in chemistry, makes the decision for the partners, based on his more thorough understanding of the standards. He agrees that he wants students to analyze, becoming more independent in their choices of safety equipment. Now Ms. Kyle can propose instructional strategies that address analysis instead of use.

Conversations like this one may require some courage. It can be awkward to ask a colleague to reconsider their plan. They may feel threatened or embarrassed, called out by someone who doesn't have the same expertise. Both parties will feel vulnerable. However, exposing our vulnerabilities builds trust and confidence, resulting in better decision making for students.

The literacy coaches in Mrs. Weissman's district have created a pacing guide for each grade level. Mrs. Weissman, a middle-school special education teacher, uses the guide to plan for the students she and her paraeducator serve in their self-contained classroom. Looking ahead, she sees that in the "objective" column for each day next week it says *write a personal narrative.*

This is a five-day writing unit that she needs to break into actionable chunks. Not only does she want her students to understand their daily learning target, she needs her paraeducator to understand the specific pieces that need to be accomplished each day.

She breaks the broader goal down into daily learning targets:

M – I can explain the characteristics of a personal narrative.
T – I can narrow my topic to a small moment in time.
W – I can generate specific details to support my topic.
Th – I can produce a rough draft of my personal narrative.
F – I can edit and revise my draft.

Mrs. Weissman feels much more confident sharing this version with her paraeducator and anyone else that might stop into her room. Even a visit from the principal will feel better if everyone can pinpoint the exact outcomes expected from the day's lesson. Mrs. Weissman decides to go one step further and create a sheet of Download Bars for her students to use each day (Figure 5.2). At the start of the lesson, they will shade in how much of this skill they feel they have already 'downloaded' into their brain, and again at the mid-lesson checkpoint and just before the bell rings. This strategy will allow them to see their progress, release some dopamine, and make changes in their learning behaviors so that they reach the target by the end of the lesson.

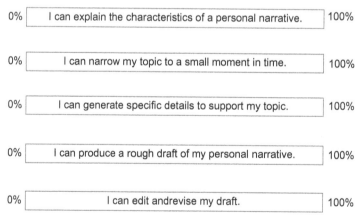

Figure 5.2 Download Bars

To Sum Up

◆ Learning targets guide learning by describing, in student-friendly language, the lesson-sized chunk of information, skills and reasoning processes that students will accomplish.
◆ Specific learning targets benefit students by clarifying the goal, allowing for self-monitoring and adjustments and increasing motivation.
◆ To develop specially designed instruction, especially for settings where adults don't work side by side, it is essential that all team members are clear on the meaning of the target. Clarifying the learning target becomes the first step in the SDI Planning Process.

Reflection Questions

◆ How do standards, goals, objectives and learning targets relate to each other? What experiences have you had with these terms?
◆ How might you help students review and make meaning of their learning target?
◆ Find a lesson plan and evaluate the learning target within it. Is it present? Is it clear? What verb is used? How might you change it?

Try This

◆ Select a school administrator to interview about the use of the terms standards, goals, objectives and targets. How do they define them? What do they see as the relationship among them?
◆ Choose a unit of study and develop daily learning targets. If the curriculum provides them, analyze each and decide if it can be clearer, be written with more student-friendly language or written more narrowly so that it can be accomplished in a single lesson.

6

Planning Steps 2 and 3: Gathering and Utilizing Information

For a recent "big" birthday, I splurged and gifted myself with a Garmin sports watch. I'd observed athletic friends and family use them for years, but never thought I needed the level of data these watches provide. After all, I wasn't trying to win podium spots. I don't consider myself coordinated, athletic or competitive. But within weeks I was hooked. My watch tracks my daily steps, my heart rate highs and lows, my sleep patterns and my activities. I can look at how fast I have walked or run each section of a mile, how many strokes I have taken in the pool and the intensity of each workout. Spending just a few minutes analyzing the data has yielded actionable results. I have been able to pinpoint my weaknesses, increase my motivation, and create workouts that make me stronger and less injury-prone.

Steps 2 and 3 of the Planning SDI process are primarily information-gathering efforts that will yield actionable results for your students. By asking the right questions early in the process, we will be able to prioritize and focus, making the most of precious minutes we have with students (Figure 6.1).

Step 2. Pinpoint the Difficult Moments Students May Experience

By asking the right questions early in the process, we will be able to prioritize and focus, making the most of precious minutes we have with students.

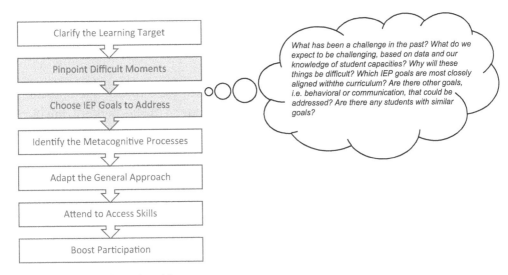

Figure 6.1 Planning Steps 2 and 3

Many experienced teachers keep notes on lessons they have taught in the past. Whether this is by using sticky notes plastered throughout the teacher manual or digital notes in an online lesson planning platform, these messages to self can save time for the teacher and improve outcomes for the students. Especially helpful are notes that say "this was hard for students" or "several struggled here." While we want to favor a strengths-based approach to addressing student needs, it is realistic to identify what will be challenging.

But what if you are teaching a new curriculum, without the benefit of experience and reflective notes? What if you are a specialist collaborating with a general education teacher to integrate SDI into something you have never taught before? A series of guiding questions can elicit valuable thought and discussion.

◆ What has been a challenge for students when this lesson was taught in the past?
◆ What might be the root cause of any difficulties?
◆ Are there foundational vocabulary terms that are necessary?
◆ Are there prerequisite skills that some students are missing?
◆ Is there a lesson component where students might get bogged down?
◆ Are there accessibility concerns for our students with disabilities?
◆ Are there lesson components that require skills such as fine-motor, visual processing or sustained attention?
◆ Is there anything that might be confusing?
◆ What does our student data tell us might be challenging?
◆ Are there moments when some students will need intensive adult intervention?

◆ Is there any other data we should look at before proceeding with our planning?

◆ What other questions does this raise?

When teachers start to feel overwhelmed by all the possible data to consider, Thomas Guskey, an internationally recognized expert on assessment, encourages us. "The best classroom assessments also serve as meaningful sources of information for teachers, helping them identify what they taught well and what they need to work on. Gathering this vital information does not require a sophisticated statistical analysis of assessment results. Teachers need only make a simple tally of how many students missed each assessment item or failed to meet a specific criterion" (2003, p. 8). In other words, simple can be enough, if we are looking at accurate information.

Pinpointing Difficult Moments in Action

The administrators at Mr. Bergstrom and Mrs. Klibanoff's school have made co-planning a priority and built schedules that allow them one period per week to meet. While grateful, they always wish they had a bit more time. They try to make the most of their forty-five minutes so that they can sketch out their five co-taught lessons for next week. Both have done a quick scan of the curriculum map and upcoming lessons in the teacher manual before arriving at the meeting. Mr. Bergstrom has added draft learning targets to each day of their online lesson planning form, and Mrs. Klibanoff has brought the IEP goals with her to their meeting.

After clarifying the learning target, "I can describe the seven roles of the President of the United States," Mrs. Klibanoff asks, "What is hard about this?"

Mr. Bergstrom explains that the lesson wasn't very successful in the past. Mrs. Klibanoff probes further with "What do you think was the root cause?"

Mr. Bergstrom explains that seven roles is a lot to remember and that some of the vocabulary terms, like Chief of State, cause students to confuse geography with government. Mrs. Klibanoff jots down "vocab" and "memory" in her notes. When she asks him about specific vocabulary terms, Mr. Bergstrom looks at his unit test item analysis and mentions four specific terms that were most often missed. When they move on to plan the meat of their lesson, they will address these challenges.

In addition to teacher recollections from past experiences, there are many sources of data that can be considered during this second step.

- Classwork
- Pre-tests
- Surveys
- Exit tickets
- Observations
- Homework
- Self-assessments
- Parent input
- Student interviews
- Short quizzes
- Show of hands
- Project work
- Student portfolios
- Behavior frequency counts
- Progress-monitoring data
- Audio and video recordings
- Standardized assessments

"Formative assessments alone do little to improve student learning or teaching quality. What really counts is what happens after the assessments" (2007, p. 28). Guskey emphasizes the connection between assessment and instruction by reminding us that what really matters is how we inform our instruction. To put this back into a sports analogy, wearing a fancy new Garmin watch does little to improve fitness if we don't adjust training based on the data. And then perhaps adjust it again, and again and maybe even again. The design process is iterative, cycling through the steps as we continue to gather information that can improve our practices.

Step 3. Choose IEP Goals to Address during the Lesson or Lesson Series

A school district in the mid-west was exploring equity issues for their students with disabilities. Data showed that students with disabilities were experiencing achievement gaps larger than the state average, no matter whether they were in general or special education settings. The leadership team and I did a walk-through of eight classrooms – four inclusive and four self-contained. As we sat around a conference table afterward to discuss our observations, one of the administrators, a strong advocate of inclusion, commented proudly that he was unable to tell which teachers in the inclusive classrooms were the specialists and which were the general educators. I held my tongue and waited to hear other comments. A special education coordinator jumped in and claimed that she didn't see the special educators in either setting doing anything that a general educator couldn't do. A principal piped up, asking "Have we been explicit enough in communicating our expectations for them to prioritize SDI?"

The role of a special educator is complex and incorporates dozens of tasks. The most important of those tasks is to provide specially designed instruction to help students meet their IEP goals. A daily mantra for a special educator should be "What IEP goals am I working on? What am I doing that is special?" If general education practices were 100% effective for students with disabilities, they would not have an IEP. Therefore, whether services are provided in separate or integrated settings, those services should look different than what you would see from a general educator. "The common misconception – that good co-teachers become clones of each other – often results in poor outcomes for students" (Beninghof 2015, p. 10). We must expect IEP goals to be alive and flourishing in all phases of instruction, but particularly in the planning phase.

> A daily mantra for a special educator should be "What IEP goals am I working on? What am I doing that is special?"

In the reauthorization of IDEA (2006) Congress removed the federal requirement for IEPs to include both annual goals and short-term objectives, except for students on alternate assessments. Some states have chosen to continue the requirement for objectives (also referred to as benchmarks), so this third step in planning will vary slightly depending on your location. For uniformity, we will use the term IEP *goal*.

Many excellent resources exist to help teachers craft high-quality IEP goals. Lisa Goran and her colleagues pose four rules for writing effective goals (2020, p. 337):

1   Be succinct, communicating the specific intent with clarity.
2   Write about the expected skill or behavior, not about the process.
3   Focus only on student needs identified in the present levels of academic achievement and functional performance (PLAAFP).
4   Add details regarding audience, target behavior, conditions under which the skill or behavior will be measured, degree of proficiency and timeline.

I would add a fifth rule or guideline: Align goals to grade-level standards with an emphasis on rigorous expectations. For example, a goal using terms like "identify" or "describe" from the lowest levels of Bloom's Taxonomy or Depths of Knowledge is much less likely to bridge an achievement gap than goals that use terms such as "apply," "analyze" or "create." Likewise, goals that reflect below-grade-level expectations will probably result in below-grade-level outcomes. Academic goals should be linked to a related grade-level standard without simply restating the standard. Instead, the goal (or the objectives/benchmarks) should address the gap, meeting the student's individual entry level with a belief in growth.

Some districts have found it helpful to consider a readiness continuum when writing goals. Let's look at a common grade-level standard for elementary language arts:

> **RL 2.9** *Compare and contrast two or more versions of the same story by different authors or cultures.*

Using a readiness or complexity continuum, we consider the individual student's unique needs and choose from several different entry points for this grade-level standard, as seen in the example in Table 6.1.

Because what is complex for one student may not be for another, team members use this type of chart to generate ideas for entry points without viewing it as a lock-step continuum. They may even need to generate an entry point not listed in order to address the student's unique level. Once the entry point has been agreed upon, goals, objectives and/or benchmarks can be written for the IEP.

Teams that follow these five rules or guidelines when writing goals will be able to generate a clear map of priorities for their students and help to close achievement gaps.

Planning Matrix

To map out the big picture, many teachers use a Planning Matrix (Beninghof and Singer 1995). A planning matrix provides an overall picture of the student's program, allowing for an easy check that all goals are being addressed throughout the course of the week. It also highlights in which periods the student will need accommodations, SDI and staffing supports. Table 6.2 shows a planning matrix for a third-grade student with significant disabilities.

To complete the matrix, team members shade periods of the school day where a goal *might* be addressed. Next they place an X in periods where a goal *will* be addressed. This means that SDI and data collection will occur during these periods. In the bottom row, teams identify how much support the student will need to be successful in each period. This form should be considered a guideline for the student's day, rather than an inflexible schedule.

Table 6.1 Example of a Complexity Continuum of Entry Points for RL2.9

Less Complex		More Complex
• Direct visual attention to a book or image… • Activate communication device to answer Y/N questions… • Sustain auditory attention to stories read aloud…	• Distinguish among items based on known similarities or differences (color, shape, texture, size)… • Identify story elements such as characters, plot… • Match images or ideas to one of two texts…	• Attend to details of a literary text… • Describe images or ideas found in a text… • Summarize the plot of a literary text… • Select the correct text based on a close-ended question…	• Identify similarities between two texts… • Select text evidence to support similarities… • Analyze text for evidence of cultural characteristics… • Analyze text for author's purpose or writing style…	• Identify differences between two texts… • Select text evidence to support differences… • Create a new version of a common text by changing several elements…

Table 6.2 Planning Matrix Example

Name: Marcus School: Best Elementary School Grade: 3 Date: August 26

REGULAR CLASS ACTIVITIES/PERIODS

Standard	IEP Goals	Check in/out	Lang. Arts	Art	Tech Media	Lunch	Math	Social Studies	Science	P.E Health	Music
3.SL3.3	Ask & answer questions		X				X				
3.RF.3.3	Identify sight words		X								
3.SL.3.6	Request breaks when needed			X						X	
3.L3.6	Be aware of social cues							X	X		
3.OA.A3	Count to 30						X				
3.SL.3.4	Categorize items			X	X						
3.RL.4	Apply prepositions		X						X	X	
3.RI.7	Identify safety practices	X									
3.SL3.1	Initiate conversation	X		X		X					
3.PE. 5.5	Awareness of personal space										X
	Participation Level	SDI IA	SDI M 2nd	SDI 2nd	S IA	S P	SDI M 2nd	S P	SDI M 2nd	A IA	M IA

S = Same A = Accommodations M = Modifications SDI = Specially Designed Instruction AL = Alternative Location

P = Peer IA = Instructional Aide 2nd = Second certified adult (Sp. Ed. T, Related Prof.) No= No extra assistance

While it might be tweaked during the year, once it is done, it should provide guidance without a lot of additional work.

Teacher-Friendly Goals at a Glance

Caseloads for specialists in the U.S. range from a handful of students to as many as fifty-five. Each state places limits on caseloads, and then each local education agency determines how many teacher positions they can fund. While no national source exists to tell us the national average caseload, it appears to be about twenty-five for special educators and well above that for related professionals such as speech/language pathologists.

No matter how many students are on a caseload, it is imperative to have a way to organize IEP goals so that they are readily accessible for lesson planning. Digging through dozens of files, paper or digital, is not time-efficient. And with all the things a specialist needs to think about throughout the day, it is highly unlikely that they will be able to remember all of the goals for each of their students. Many teachers have found the Goals at a Glance forms, Tables 6.3 and 6.4, to be helpful tools. In Table 6.3 the special educator enters only the goals that are related to accessing that period's curriculum. This approach is typically used by secondary teachers. In Table 6.4, typically used at the elementary level, the special educator organizes goals by major content areas, especially if the students will receive the majority of their instruction in an inclusive setting. Some educators choose to add an additional column for accommodations. Experience suggests that no matter how many columns, keeping it all to one page will guarantee that it remains a user-friendly document.

Once a Goals at a Glance form is in place, we choose which IEP goals will be addressed for a given lesson. A series of guiding questions can lead to a sound decision.

- Which goals are most closely aligned with the curriculum for this lesson?
- Which goals will fit most seamlessly?
- Are there foundational goals or prerequisite skills that can be pre-taught at the start of the lesson?
- Does the data point to a priority?
- Will working on certain goals in this lesson better prepare students for lessons in the near future?
- Given the methods or planned activities, are certain goals easier to address?
- Are there other goals, i.e. behavioral or communication, that are relevant?

Table 6.3 Goals at a Glance by Period

Student	IEP Goals in Brief
Tamika	• Attend to and follow multi-step directions • Choose and use correct tools for graphing • Translate word stories into equations • Compare qualitative and quantitative features of a graph • Increase fluency with multiplication
Justin	• Select and use tools to find definitions • Apply mathematical terms accurately • Select and use memorization strategies
Terrance	• Use a planner to track assignments • Organize math work in a legible format • Increase attention/perseverance to complete in-class assignments
Summer	• Create mnemonics to assist with memorization • Select and use a visual organizer to assist in memorizing • Determine assignment details to add to planner
Maddee	• Advocate with teacher for preferred accommodations • Adapt to unexpected change by using strategies
Wyatt	• Attend to and follow multi-step directions • Use a graphing calculator • Apply mathematical terms accurately
Jimmy	• Grasp and place items from desk into backpack • Make eye contact with peers during conversation • Use device to answer Yes, No questions related to curriculum • Identify numerals 0–9, demonstrate 1:1 correspondence
Armando	• Apply test-taking strategies • Proof-read work and tests before handing in • Select and use strategies to decrease test anxiety

◆ Are there any students with similar goals so that some efficiency of instruction may occur?
◆ Are there goals that haven't been addressed recently and need to be?
◆ Is this the only time when this goal can be addressed this week?
◆ How might we utilize the various adults in the room so that several goals can be addressed during the lesson?

Table 6.4 Goals at a Glance by Classroom/Area

Area	Student	IEP Goals/Benchmarks in Brief
Language Arts	Hector	• Apply phonics skills to decode words • Apply phonics skills to spell words • Distinguish between words with similar meanings or spellings • Increase reading fluency
	Hannah	• Identify letter names within text • Apply phonics skills to decode initial sounds • Demonstrate understanding of basic text principles • Ask/answer open-ended questions about text • Use technology to compose simple sentences
	George	• Apply phonics skills to decode words • Apply phonics skills to spell words
	Zack	• Write complete sentences within paragraphs • Create an explanatory text with clear main idea • Sequence events accurately in writing
Math	Hector	• Create drawings and equations to represent math problems • Justify choices of math strategies
	Marciella	• Represent and solve addition/subtraction problems • Identify and use place value with 2 digits • Represent and interpret data • Compare measurable attributes using correct terms
	Hannah	• Identify numerals 0–9 • Input numbers and addition sign on large calculator • Determine measurable attributes of a group of objects • Select and use technology tools to collect data
	George	• Engage in math discussion with peers using grade-level content terms

(Continued)

Area	Student	IEP Goals/Benchmarks in Brief
Social Emotional	George	• Transition quickly between activities • Preview and follow individual schedule • Express emotions to adults through speech
	Zak	• Identify and use problem-solving strategies for social situations • Select and use strategies to decrease impulsivity • Increase length of on-task behavior
Other	George	• Display speech fluency • Select and use word retrieval strategies
	Hannah	• Improve pencil grip stamina • Self-monitor and strengthen sitting posture

IEP Goals in Action

Mr. Bergstrom and Mrs. Klibanoff continue with their planning discussion. She opens the Goals at a Glance document for their co-taught period and the two teachers take a quick look. She immediately sees a few goals related to memorization and vocabulary acquisition. After mentioning them to her partner, they agree to embed those into the lesson. In addition, Mr. Bergstrom suggests that they can address a few of the language goals by setting up some small group discussion opportunities into which Mrs. Klibanoff can incorporate SDI. After spending just a minute or two on this step, they are ready to move forward with their planning process.

A clever meme surfaces from time to time on social media channels. The letters IEP fill most of the screen, but underneath them are the words "I expect progress." When we intentionally choose goals, we position ourselves and our students at the start line, at the front of the pack, ready to move forward. We expect progress based on our careful planning. To paraphrase writer and poet Kahlil Gibran, progress lies not just in supporting what is, but in advancing toward what will be.

To Sum Up

◆ Gathering information before planning the lesson adaptations will ensure that instruction is focused and prioritized.

◆ Many useful sources of information exist. Depending on the learning target, you will choose to analyze different sources to determine where challenges and pitfalls hide so that you can proactively tackle them.

◆ A special educator's primary responsibility is to provide specially designed instruction. In order to do this, IEP goals need to be clearly written, readily accessible and intentionally chosen. Every day, a special educator should ask, "What IEP goals am I working on in this lesson?"

Reflection Questions

◆ Mr. Bergstrom and Mrs. Klibanoff discuss these second and third steps in just a few minutes. How might you build efficiency into the early stages of your lesson planning?

◆ How do you make IEP goals user-friendly and easily accessible for planning? Have you seen others use a different organizational system?

◆ Recall a lesson you have taught or observed recently. What IEP goals were embedded into the lesson? What IEP goals could have been embedded?

Try This

◆ Search the internet for suggestions from special educators on how to organize IEP goals for ease of use. Compare various ideas and create a format that includes the best of each.

◆ Find an article on time management strategies. Which of the ideas seems applicable to a SDI planning meeting? Try one or two and reflect on their impact.

7

Planning Step 4: Identify the Metacognitive Process that a Successful Learner Might Use

A few months ago, I decided to enhance my outdoor running routine by doing fartlek. Fartlek, which means 'speed play' in Swedish, is the process of mixing up faster periods of running with slower periods of running or walking. I warmed up a bit, jogged slowly to the first light pole, then did an all-out sprint to the next light pole. Sometimes I ran to a fire hydrant or parked car, but always varied the speed from fast to slow. When sprinting, I had to really concentrate on the pavement and my solid foot placement. Near the end of my workout, tired physically and mentally, I stopped concentrating just long enough to trip, with several scrapes and bruises resulting from my inattention.

While I consider myself clumsier than average, most of us have tripped on the stairs, stepped awkwardly off a curb or stumbled over an unnoticed object. We often follow this by saying, "I wasn't paying attention. I was thinking about _____ (what to eat for dinner, the movie we watched, a conversation I had, etc.)" We stop thinking about the actions we are taking and end up embarrassed, injured or unable to accomplish our goal.

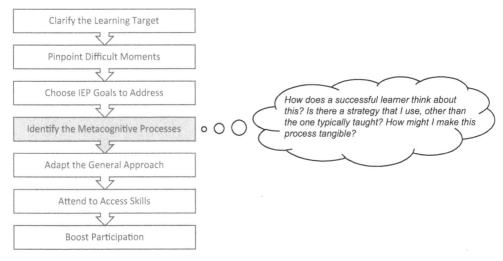

Figure 7.1 Planning Step 4

What Is Metacognition?

Metacognition, often referred to as thinking about our thinking, is a broad term that refers to a person's awareness of how they think and learn. Foreign language teacher Rachel Poth explains that metacognition allows us to "understand ourselves in the whole process of learning and can develop skills to think about, connect with, and evaluate our learning and interactions each day" (October 6, 2019). The ability to understand ourself is a first step toward understanding others. Effective teachers have a strong grasp on their own learning processes and preferences and can then put themselves in someone else's shoes. While those shoes may not be a perfect fit for the teacher, they might be a perfect fit for one or more students. When teachers can understand their own thinking and their students' thinking, then they are primed for successful learning experiences.

Researcher John Hattie agrees, saying "metacognitive skills are one of the ultimate goals of all learning" (2012, p. 115). Adults with strong metacognitive skills can think through a problem, consider and choose from alternative strategies and reflectively evaluate the outcome. This is a perfect match for what specialists need to do in order to implement SDI! To avoid stumbling, we want to attend to our thinking and learning processes. As educator Julie Landvogt says, "in order for schools to be places of thinking for children, they must also be places of thinking for adults" (2011, p. 234). Not only is teacher thinking a key skill to be developed during pre-service programs, it needs ongoing opportunities and attention. The busy teacher feels a constant pressure to move forward with the pacing, to multi-task during team meetings and to save time by just following the teacher's guide. School leaders can promote more time for teacher thinking and metacognitive practices by adding a few practice minutes to their staff meetings or Professional Learning Community (PLC) agendas (Prytula 2012). Leaders can also articulate the benefits – that pausing to ask metacognitive questions during planning saves time in future re-teaching. Additionally, leaders can share research showing that teachers who reflect about their own practices and value thinking over pacing have classes of students who are more thoughtful (Onosko 1992).

Is metacognition easy? Some people are naturally more reflective and find it easy to think about their thinking. Many of the day-to-day problems people face are well-defined with limited duration and known solutions. Teaching does not fall within those parameters. Instead, researchers Lin, Schwartz and Hatano remind us that "Teaching has unique qualities that differentiate it from many of the tasks and environments that metacognitive interventions have supported. Teachers often confront highly variable situations" (2005, p. 245). They suggest that teachers benefit most by using *adaptive metacognition*, which involves being able to change thinking in response to a wide range of variables. Even apparently routine classroom activities have numerous variables because teaching is such a social interaction. This is amplified in an inclusive classroom, where we have an even wider readiness range and are committed to addressing the unique needs of students with disabilities.

Consider the apparently simple routine of entering a classroom and taking an assigned seat. In an inclusive setting, the teachers may need adaptive metacognition to think about:

◆ Samuel's need to distance himself from perceived germs on furniture or peers.
◆ Chung's preferences for furniture that remains unmoved due to his low vision and mobility issues.
◆ Adeline's visual distractibility as she enters an overwhelmingly busy room.
◆ Jeffrey's perception that directions are always a negative, authoritarian control of his freedoms.
◆ Justine's social circle, viewed by her as a protective, life-saving group of friends that cannot be ignored.

And these are just a fraction of the individual student variables! Add to this mix the adult variables, interpersonal, environmental and curriculum variables and we can clearly see why step four in this process is crucial.

Metacognition Self-Assessment

How honed are your metacognitive skills? Because we are exploring how to plan for SDI, let's look specifically at metacognitive skills that fall within the planning phase. These skills include goal information management, comprehension monitoring, debugging and evaluation. Use the self-assessment in Table 7.1 to examine your current skillset.

There is an abundance of research that proves adults and children can improve their metacognition through observation, awareness and training in strategies. No matter what your self-assessment score, a growth mindset is warranted. Try one or more of the following activities to boost your skills.

◆ Observe other teachers' think alouds with students. Compare them to your own metacognitive process.
◆ Ask team members to share their thinking with you. Follow up with questions that take a deeper dive into the thinking process rather than just the outcome.
◆ Practice taking on the perspective of a specific student. How might they think about this? Then switch to another student's perspective.
◆ Delay your processing of a just-read text or curriculum guide. Research shows that pausing before summarizing causes a reader to comprehend more fully, rather than just recall isolated information (Anderson and Thiede 2008). Teachers who scan upcoming lessons can then ruminate on them over time.
◆ Retake the Metacognition Self-Assessment every few months. By reading through the statements regularly, you will be practicing metacognition and reminding yourself of the most important skills.

Metacognition in Action

Second graders in Mr. Booker's class are immersed in literacy throughout the day. His bookshelves are stocked with quality fiction and non-fiction books as well as magazines, newspapers and other print material. His love of history means he has incorporated text material that represents many cultures, time periods and geographic regions. Most of the students are making good progress through the district-selected literacy curriculum. But Mr. Booker and the special education teacher, Mrs. Gallagher, frequently adapt the lessons for a few students who need something different. At today's planning meeting, they have already identified the following:

Table 7.1 Metacognition Self-Assessment

Directions: Check True or False for each statement about yourself.

Regulation of Cognition	True	False
1 I think about what I really need to learn before I begin a task.		
2 I ask myself questions about the material before I begin.		
3 I slow down when I encounter important information.		
4 I consciously focus my attention on important information.		
5 I focus on the meaning and significance of new information.		
6 I create my own examples too make information more meaningful.		
7 I draw pictures or diagrams to help me understand.		
8 I try to translate new information into my own words.		
9 I try to break down new learning into smaller steps.		
10 I focus on overall meaning rather than specifics.		
11 I change strategies when I fail to understand.		
12 I re-evaluate my assumptions when I get confused.		
13 I consider several alternatives before I choose.		
14 I ask myself if I have considered all options when solving a problem.		
15 I periodically review to help me understand important relationships.		
16 I find myself pausing regularly to check my comprehension.		
17 I view the issue from someone else's perspective.		
18 I look for relationships among components.		
Scoring: 1 point for every True statement, 0 pts. for every False statement		
TOTAL	/18	

Adapted from the Metacognitive Awareness Inventory (MAI) Open Source Document, Schraw, G. & Dennison, R.S. (1994)

1   Lesson Target: *I can evaluate my writing to determine which text features to add to support my readers.*
2   Difficult moments: rushing ahead, choosing first feature on anchor chart, choosing favorite text feature, choosing simplest text feature
3   IEP Goals: provide details, produce complete sentences, capitalize first word in sentence, attend to task, follow classroom rules, modulate voice volume

The teachers look at the anchor chart provided with the curriculum (Figure 7.2).

Mrs. Gallagher asks, "What would go through your head if you were trying to decide what text features to add to a piece of your own writing?" They both intentionally pause to think.

Mr. Booker is a prolific writer, doing guest blog posts for a number of Civil War websites. He speaks first. "I usually scan my work to see what pops out at me. If I noticed that I've used a lot of dates, I'd probably consider adding a timeline. It's the process of scanning that shows me patterns or frequencies and then I decide."

Mrs. Gallagher replies, "In essence, you do the opposite of what the anchor chart leads students to do. You don't look at the text feature first. Instead you look at your writing first." Their awareness causes them to develop two ways of teaching the lesson – the way the curriculum presents the text features

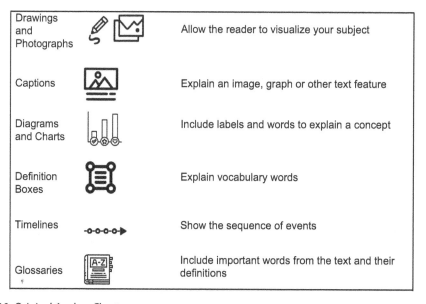

Figure 7.2 Original Anchor Chart

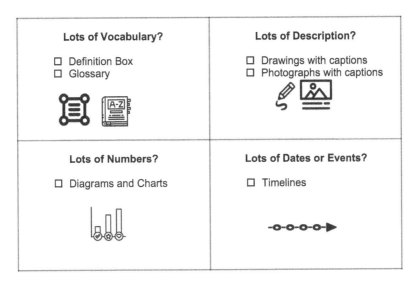

Figure 7.3 Alternative Anchor Chart

first, and a way to scan the writing first to see what pops out. An alternative anchor chart easily flows from their discussion (Figure 7.3).

The following questions can guide you to find alternative solutions to the typical general education approach. Remember, if the general education approach is working for students with IEPs, then you won't need specially designed instruction or adaptive metacognition. IEP goals are designed to meet the gap that occurs when the general education approach isn't working for these students. Special educators must be able to envision alternative approaches, consider various scenarios and put themselves in their learners' shoes.

Guiding Questions for Metacognition

- ◆ How does a successful learner think about this?
- ◆ Is there a strategy that I use, other than the one typically taught?
- ◆ What goes on in my head as I consider this?
- ◆ Why does this approach make sense? Not make sense?
- ◆ What are the inherent distinctions, relationships, organizational systems or perspectives?
- ◆ How might I make this process tangible?
- ◆ Is this similar to a previous task?
- ◆ What prior knowledge will help with this?
- ◆ How does this relate to student life?
- ◆ What personal connections can be made?

- ◆ Are there any metaphors that would amplify their understanding?
- ◆ Is there a more rigorous way to think about it? A simpler way?

Mrs. Lopez is driving home from school with a nagging headache. Her Algebra course is mostly problem-based lessons that students work through in collaborative study teams. Productive struggle is a theme she returns to frequently with students, guiding them to figure things out for themselves. It is some of the related behaviors that are causing her headache today. Even though she posts directions on the board, reviews them with the class and encourages students to ask each other for assistance, she has a few teens that constantly call out, "Mrs. Lopez, what do we do next? Mrs. Lopez, can you help us? Mrs. Lopez, come over here." Because some have IEP goals related to memory and following directions, she tallied these behaviors over the last week and is discouraged by their frequency.

As she drives, she wonders why they can't remember to look at the board or their books for directions or to ask their peers for help. Her sister, a third-grade teacher, has shared that she teaches her students the rhyme, "ask three before me." Mrs. Lopez worries that using this may feel a bit too elementary for her older teen students. However, the idea of a mnemonic appeals to her. She could create one and give it to students to help them remember what to do. A few blocks later she has an "Aha" moment. She thinks, "Instead of giving them a mnemonic, I could teach them the process for creating a mnemonic. We could apply it to this problem and then they could use the new skill whenever they need to remember something." Happy with this solution, she sets her mind to identifying the steps in creating a mnemonic.

The next day in class, Mrs. Lopez reviews what a mnemonic is and asks students to share any mnemonics they know. She hears HOMES, PEMDAS, *Every Good Boy Does Fine* and a few other familiar devices. Next, she thinks aloud as she explains to students her metacognition about how she creates mnemonics to help her remember things. Mrs. Lopez labels the steps and guides them through the current classroom issue of students needing to work more independently.

1 Identify what you want to remember. (Students decide on three things: reread directions in Algebra book, look at anchor charts, ask a teammate.)
2 Shorten to key words. (Students choose book, look, team.)
3 Arrange into a new word or memorable phrase. (Students latch onto BLT.)

Mrs. Lopez loves that students thought of a BLT and quickly searches for an online image of a BLT to add to the bullet points they are generating on the slide. For the remainder of the lesson, if a student calls out, Mrs. Lopez calls back – "Use your BLT strategy!"

Of course, she realizes that the students will need repeated practice with creating mnemonics, as well as opportunities to apply the process in several contexts before it will become second nature for them. But she is pleased that her own metacognition led to a plan for specially designed instruction. She did more than just give them a mnemonic tool – she instructed them on how to create their own, so that they will become more independent in their learning.

Let's look at the Guiding Questions for SDI that help us determine if Mrs. Lopez's approach is SDI.

◆ Is it special? Something different from the typical general education practices?

   While general education teachers may provide mnemonics to students, it is not typical of them to teach students how to create a mnemonic.

◆ Does it address the child's unique needs?

   Testing had identified a few students that had reduced working memory along with their specific learning disabilities.

◆ Is it related to an IEP goal? Are we collecting data for progress monitoring?

   Mrs. Lopez collected frequency data on the behavior and will continue to do so. She will also collect data on how successful the students become at creating mnemonics on their own.

◆ Is it instruction rather than a tool or accommodation?

   Instead of just giving students a BLT mnemonic, she taught them how to create mnemonics. The skill is much more likely to generalize to a variety of settings.

◆ Is it intentional? Designed to bring about progress?

   This strategy was thought out in advance (driving home counts!) and designed to create more independence for her students. She expects to see progress on related IEP goals and will monitor it over the coming weeks.

◆ Is it growing a skill that will be transferrable or generalizable?

   Teens with strong study skills will be more successful in a variety of content areas. In addition, Mrs. Lopez is familiar with the research that says that metacognitive strategies learned in one domain help increase the speed of learning in other domains.

◆ Is it building independence?

Awareness of self leads to opportunities for independence. By modeling and guiding a metacognitive strategy, Mrs. Lopez not only provided students with a memory trick but also with a map that will lead to greater independence.

> Each time teachers practice applying metacognition to their SDI planning, the technique will become stronger, faster and more natural.

As I shared at the beginning of this chapter, I took a tumble while running and ended up with several scrapes and bruises. The next few times I went for a run, my concentration was at an all-time high, being very aware of every divot and bump in the road. It took a fair amount of energy to think about how I was planting each foot. With each successive run, my technique became stronger, my times got faster, and my foot placement felt more natural. Each time teachers practice applying metacognition to their SDI planning, the technique will become stronger, faster and more natural, helping everyone reach the IEP goal finish line.

To Sum Up

◆ Metacognition is a broad term that refers to a person's awareness of how they think and learn.
◆ Children and adults can be taught to improve their strategic metacognitive skills.
◆ SDI Planning Step 4, identifying the metacognitive processes, can lead to several solid alternative methods for adapting instruction. Not everyone thinks the same way. In order to address the IEP goals, the special educator will need to generate different approaches.

Reflection Questions

◆ What is a situation, unrelated to school, in which you have used adaptive metacognition?
◆ How often do you model authentic think alouds, using your own personal experiences rather than those given by the curriculum writers?
◆ Which of the guiding questions for metacognition struck you as the most helpful? Why?

Try This

- As you engage in a task, consider the thinking process you are using. Ask at least two other adults how they would think about that same task. For example, "How would you analyze two different news accounts of the same event?"
- Choose three of the guiding questions, print them and keep them in this book or open on your device as you continue to read. Review them each time you finish a chapter and take time to think about your thinking.

8

Planning Step 5:
Adapt the General Approach

Walk any distance on nature trails at high elevation or in rocky areas and you are likely to encounter cairns. Cairns, man-made piles of stones, have been used since prehistoric times as landmarks, monuments, places of safe-keeping and ceremonial tools. Most recently, rock balancing has become a popular artistic expression of play, fun or meditation. Those who build cairns are able to examine the stones, choose ones that have synergy of shape and transform a loose collection of rocks into a beautiful pillar with a new purpose. This transformation relies on the strength of what was already there, but converts it into a new expression.

In Step 5 of the SDI Planning Process, special educators and related professionals create ways to adapt or transform a lesson so that students with disabilities will find it accessible and be successful. The term "adapt" is used in the legislation, but the term "transformation" is more accurate to the experience of implementing specially designed instruction. Our goal should be to create a change that addresses the unique needs, yet still integrates the original standard that applies to all students (Figure 8.1).

> Adapt v. to make something suitable for a new use or purpose.
> Transform v. a process by which one thing is converted into another that is equivalent in some important aspect but is differently expressed.

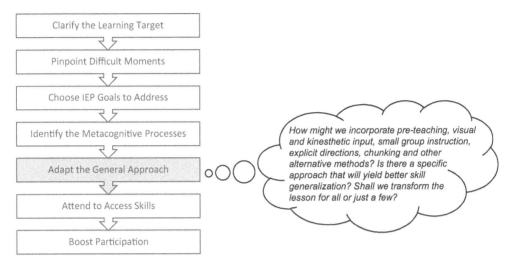

Figure 8.1 Planning Step 5

Adapting Instruction

All teachers have experience with making adaptations to help students achieve goals. They have provided tools such as graphic organizers, talk stems, color-coded pages and more. These general accommodations are helpful, but are different from the adapting process that is required for specially designed instruction. (See definition in Chapter 3.) As John Hoover and James Patton, experts in English language development, tell us "Examples of practices that fall within general curriculum – increased wait time, cooperative learning, extra time to build background knowledge, alternate assessments – these do not constitute specially designed instruction and are not acceptable reasons for requiring a special education label in order to receive them. EL Learners should not need to have an IEP in order to expect these accommodations and changes to content or methodology" (2017, p. 103). Let's go further and say that NO student should require a special education label in order to receive these types of accommodations.

When we reflect back on the Guiding Questions for SDI found in Chapter 3, we can begin to distinguish general education practices from specially designed instruction:

Guiding Questions for SDI

◆ Is it special? Something different from the typical general education practices?
◆ Does it address the child's unique needs?

- Is it related to an IEP goal? Are we collecting data for progress monitoring?
- Is it instruction rather than a tool or accommodation?
- Is it intentional? Designed to bring about progress?
- Is it growing a skill that will be transferrable or generalizable?
- Is it building independence?

Research-Based Practices

In addition to these characteristics, specialists are given a legal mandate under IDEA that instruction should be based on peer-reviewed research (PRR) to the extent practicable (20 U.S.C., 1414[d][1aiIV]). Policy expert Mitchell Yell recommends, "Teachers should be prepared to discuss… and be able to explain the research behind the educational strategies and procedures in the services they have provided or will provide" (2013). To support special educators in this endeavor, the Council for Exceptional Children (CEC) has identified a set of high-leverage practices (HLPs) based on the following criteria:

- Focus directly on instructional practice.
- Occur with high frequency in teaching.
- Research-based and known to foster important kinds of student engagement and learning.
- Broadly applicable and usable in any content area or approach to teaching.
- So important that skillfully executing them is fundamental to effective teaching.

While all twenty-two HLPs are important for special educators, nine of them relate most directly to Step 5 of the SDI Planning Process (Table 8.1).

In addition to the research-based practices that CEC has identified, other organizations have also curated resources. The U.S. Department of Education established the What Works Clearinghouse (WWC) in 2002, whose mission is to review the research, determine which studies meet rigorous standards, and summarize the findings. This searchable database includes literacy, mathematics and behavior studies, but also includes information on interventions for students with disabilities (https://ies.ed.gov/ncee/wwc/FWW).

Moreover, the best special educators actively seek out information relevant to their specific jobs. One special education teacher may need proven practices related to students with dyslexia, while her colleague across the

Table 8.1 Selected High-Leverage Practices

Action	Description	PRR Examples
Systematically design instruction toward a specific learning goal	Logical sequencing of lesson components, activating prior knowledge, connecting lessons, adequate time allocation	• Specific lesson targets shared with students • Advance organizers • Content exposure followed by visual displays
Adapt curriculum tasks and materials for specific learning goals	Selection of materials and technology, adjustment to content quantity and success criteria, choosing meaningful tasks	• Task analysis • Memory enhancing strategies • Guided notes
Teach cognitive and metacognitive strategies to support learning and independence	Explicit instruction in executive function skills metacognitive strategies and self-monitoring	• Self-monitoring • Text interaction strategies • Self-regulated strategy development (SRSD)
Provide scaffolded supports	Provision of temporary supports calibrated to student's current level, evaluation of their effectiveness, fading and removal for independence	• Models of completed tasks • Visual representations • Reciprocal teaching
Use explicit instruction	Explicit modeling of tasks through visual and verbal supports, intentional choice of examples, anticipated misconceptions, removal of distracting information	• New content in small steps • Guided practice • Massed and distributed independent practice

(Continued)

Table 8.1 (Continued)

Action	Description	PRR Examples
Use assistive and instructional technologies	Select, implement and evaluate various technologies that aid student learning, instruct on use to grow independence	• Video self-modeling • Augmentative and alternative communication systems • Computer-aided instruction for cognitive skills
Provide intensive instruction	Match intensity of instruction to student need. Determine size and composition of small groups for maximum learning opportunity	• Immediate, corrective feedback • Significantly more practice opportunities • Integrated content instruction with executive function strategies
Teach students to maintain and generalize new learning across time and settings	Use instructional methods that promote learning transfer to other settings, people, time or materials, increase access in unknown situations	• Training sufficient exemplars • Identifying common features • Communication training for generalization
Provide positive and constructive feedback to guide students' learning and behavior	Deliver feedback that is specific, timely, contingent, age-appropriate and goal-related, assist student to receive and apply feedback effectively	• Relating feedback to the goal • Feedback as questioning • Teaching error identification skills

hall may need research on autism. Fortunately, several professional associations produce journals and books filled with the most recent findings of what works in various specialties. Teachers who keep abreast of the latest information can then use this knowledge to adapt lessons so their students will experience success.

Adapting in Action

Notice how the specialist in the following scenario, Mrs. Mendoza, uses her knowledge of proven practices to transform a writing lesson.

MRS. NEVIN: Next week we will be working on writing a personal narrative.

MRS. MENDOZA: What is the biggest struggle students have with this?

MRS. NEVIN: They can't seem to narrow their topic enough to add detail. For example, in a three-paragraph piece, they will try to write about their entire Disney vacation.

MRS. MENDOZA: Teresa, Kyle and Cheng have IEP goals about adding detail to their writing. They can't add much detail if they keep their topic too broad. Perhaps we can show them how to chunk it or narrow it. Chunking is an evidenced-based practice for content delivery, and I think we could apply it here. What if we modeled chunking through a clock approach? Let me show you what I mean.

Mrs. Mendoza quickly sketches out the following illustrations (Figure 8.2)

MRS. MENDOZA: We can walk students through a twelve-hour portion of a Saturday when they went to a birthday party. We could then ask them to pick the one hour that might be most interesting to write about. Next we can give them a one-hour clock broken down into fifteen-minute intervals, where they can identify the major activities of each interval. Finally, they can pick which is most interesting as their focus.

MRS. NEVIN: And if we chunk our instruction so that we give them the big picture, then everyone does the twelve-hour clock for their own topic, we process as a whole group, then we move to the one-hour clock…

MRS. MENDOZA: Sure. Our flow map could look like this (Figure 8.3):

When we look back at the guiding questions for SDI, we can see that this instructional approach qualifies. It is instruction that is different than the norm, linked to IEP goals, and can lead to a generalizable skill. It is also evidence-based. In this co-taught example, teachers are choosing to share the strategy with all the students, even though it only counts as SDI for those with relevant IEP goals. The other students will experience incidental benefit. The teaching partners have also decided to incorporate small-group instruction so that they can better address the individual needs of some of their students. This decision powers up the strategy as it allows them to intensify support where it is needed most.

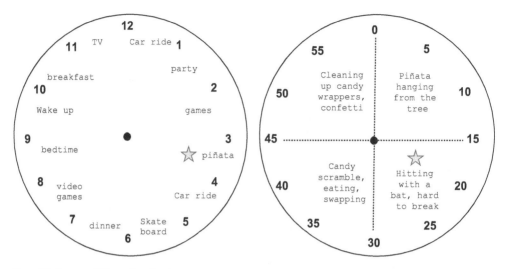

Figure 8.2 Personal Narrative Clock

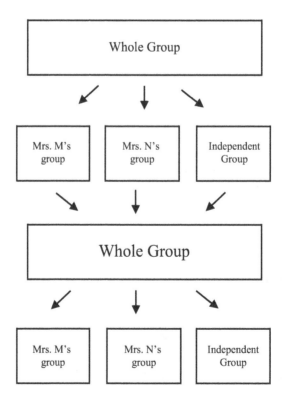

Figure 8.3 Flow Map

Do adaptations have to be major in order to qualify as SDI? Do they have to fully transform a lesson? Absolutely not. SDI can happen in shorter bursts of time and be less obvious. In Mr. Williams' U.S. Government class, students were falling behind in notetaking during his lectures. He and his special education partner, Miss Bali, discussed offering certain students partially completed notes. While Miss Bali realized that an accommodation like this might be helpful, she also wanted to approach the problem from an SDI angle. Was there a missing skill that she could address? The partners discussed the problem in more depth and hypothesized that several students didn't know how to abbreviate. A few of these students had IEP goals related to notetaking and study skills.

Miss Bali offered to design a micro-lesson on abbreviating and weave it into their next class. She explained her idea to Mr. Williams.

MISS BALI: When you use a lengthy word in your lecture, I'll jump in and ask students to talk with peers about how they might abbreviate it. I'll write their suggestions on the board and direct students to look for patterns. I'll point out a strategy for abbreviating, like using the first syllable. As the lecture continues, I'll listen for another lengthy word from you, pausing the class to practice again.

Miss Bali will analyze student notes prior to this intervention and in the weeks following, so she can see if her instruction is bringing about progress. If not, she might decide to do more intensive, one-on-one instruction or to switch interventions. Progress monitoring data will help her to be very intentional with her SDI.

Another fruitful area for adapting instruction involves adding movement. There is a solid base of evidence on the connection between movement and learning. Movement has been shown to increase alertness, memory and student achievement. Movement also elevates energy, improves mood and can increase concentration. With all of these benefits, specialists will want to consider movement as a possible adaptation. However, adding movement *does not always* transform it into specially designed instruction. Movement itself is not special. Any teacher might ask students to stand up in response to a question or walk up to a chart on the walls. In specially designed instruction, movement is added very intentionally to address the IEP goal and develop the missing skill. Movement might be small or gross motor, while seated at a desk or while working at a job training site. It might involve manipulatives, hand gestures or a total physical response. No matter the nature of the movement, in order for it to be considered SDI, it must be linked to the unique needs of a student as represented in their IEP.

Raymond was a gregarious, active twelve-year-old whose presence in any classroom was always obvious. Not only did he frequently get out of his seat to take an in-class field trip, but he also dominated any conversation. Raymond had not yet learned to turn-take in discussions; instead, he impulsively adds his own thoughts whenever they entered his head. His team had identified this as a growing problem, affecting his peer relationships and teachers' patience. A communication goal was added to his IEP – *Raymond will monitor and regulate his verbal contributions in small-group discussions, offering no more than twice the contributions of his peers' average.*

Mr. Packard, Raymond's special education teacher, was a patient man with a capacity-focused mindset. He frequently added movement to his instruction and encouraged students to advocate for their movement needs. Some of his students sat on therapy balls while others had fidgets to keep their hands busy. Because of the success he saw when adding movement, he wanted to approach Raymond's communication goal with something tactile or kinesthetic. Mr. Packard was also familiar with research that supports the use of visual representations. Combining these ideas, Mr. Packard created an instructional strategy he dubbed "Conversation Cubes."

When a lesson called for small-group discussion, Mr. Packard would grab a box of colorful stacking cubes (often used in math classes). He placed students into groups of four, with each student receiving either twelve red, twelve blue, twelve yellow or twelve green cubes. He explained to students that when the first student contributed to the discussion, he should stack one of his cubes in the middle of the table, starting a single tower for the group. As each of the other group members contributed to the conversation, they should take one of their cubes and add it to the tower.

Mr. Packard then directed the students to get started on their collaborative project. After a few minutes had passed, he directed everyone to pause and analyze their tower. "Should it be red, blue, yellow, green, red, blue, yellow, green?" The students felt that was too stiff – not authentic conversation. "Should it be red, red, yellow, red, blue, red, green?" Probably not. As the students learned how to analyze the visual representation of their conversation, Raymond began to notice how his contributions were dominating. This increased awareness helped motivate Raymond to give his teammates a chance to contribute.

Because students need multiple repetitions to learn a new skill, Mr. Packard used the conversation cubes for several weeks. However, he wanted Raymond to be able to generalize the skill to other settings without cubes. Mr. Packard created a phasing-out plan, moving from using concrete cubes to drawing boxes with colored markers. After a successful transition to a two-dimensional record, the special educator had students write down contributors' initials in a column. Now Raymond had a way that he could monitor his contributions in any setting.

Mr. Packard adapted his lessons to include a focus on the access skill that Raymond was missing. He incorporated a strategy often referred to as CRA – concrete-representational-abstract instruction. CRA has been proven effective in a variety of math topics, such as using algebra tiles to teach certain algebraic concepts. (Rodgers and Weiss 2019, p. 279). If algebra tiles and CRA are already part of the general education teacher's repertoire, then it is not an adaptation, not SDI. Instead, it is high-quality instruction and might be enough for the student with disabilities to be successful. If the student needs more, then special educators step in with creative ways to make it "special."

Adapting for Students on Alternate Standards

What about the student who is on alternate standards in an inclusive classroom? This is a common question of general and special education teachers. How do we provide SDI in a classroom where the student with the IEP is working on skills that are several grades below everyone else? At first glance it may seem impossible to adapt a high school algebra class for a student who is learning to add single-digit numbers. However, when we shift our perspective, possibilities readily appear.

Read aloud the following statement:

> *Look at the lesson for ALL that it offers, not just its traditionally intended purpose.*

This mantra can help shift teachers' perspectives when trying to meaningfully include a student with different standards and goals. Take Heather, a friendly teenager with a contagious smile. Heather also happens to have a significant intellectual disability, language and motor deficits. Her math goals include:

◆ Heather will demonstrate understanding of one-to-one correspondence by accurately counting out materials for distribution up to 20.
◆ Heather will add single digits with 90% accuracy using TouchMath® strategies.

It may seem to some that Heather would be wasting her time in an algebra class. Her team thought differently! Using a Planning Matrix (see Chapter 6, Table 6.2), they mapped out a typical week and identified which periods of the day would lend themselves to addressing Heather's unique needs. The team realized that she had several goals, in addition to her math goals, that could be addressed in algebra class, including:

- Heather will verbally interact with peers using complete sentences, at least twice per class period.
- Heather will grasp objects with her dominant hand and transfer them from one surface to another 9/10 trials.
- Heather will increase her sight words from 24 to 36.
- Heather will follow two-step directions in group settings when verbally prompted to listen closely and when task is within her skill level.

Let's imagine an algebra class and repeat our mantra, *"Look at the lesson for ALL that it offers, not just its traditionally intended purpose."* With this perspective, we see the richness of classroom materials, the range of opportunities during active instruction and the social interactions that can be structured to support Heather. We might have Heather do one or more of the following:

- Count how many students are in Rows 1 and 2.
- Count out and distribute materials to those students.
- Count how many students have their hand up in response to a teacher's question.
- Search her math textbook for some of her sight words, such as "directions, stop, add, count, find and choose."
- Follow a two-step direction to get her materials and join a group.
- Join a group doing a math exploration and engage in conversation using complete sentences.
- Respond to a teacher's question using a complete sentence.
- Answer a single-digit addition question from the teacher as they model an equation on the board.
- Circle specific words or numbers on a worksheet intended for algebra equations.

These are just a few examples of how opportunities expand when we stop looking at just the intended purpose of the algebra lesson. With this more open mindset, the special educator chooses one or more goals for which she will provide SDI during a given period.

Heather's special education teacher, Mrs. Prescott, chooses to focus her instruction on the one-to-one correspondence goal. She knows from assessing Heather that her errors occur most commonly between four and five, and fourteen and fifteen, throwing off the rest of her counting. She hypothesizes that the problem is caused by the two sequential numbers that begin with "f." Once she has clarified this in her mind (steps one through three in our SDI Planning Process) she is ready to consider the metacognitive process and make adaptations.

Mrs. Prescott reflects on her own process for counting out items. Depending on the item, she often counts by twos or fives. She wonders if chunking numbers might help Heather move through her common stumbling place. She decides to have Heather practice counting items in groups of three, so that the numbers four, five and six run fluidly together. Mrs. Prescott also decides to just focus on single-digit fluidity first; when Heather has had repeated success, they will move on to the teens.

During her next co-planning session, Mrs. Prescott tells her algebra partner that she would like Heather to be assigned as "materials captain" for her team. While students are settling into class and getting out their homework, Mrs. Prescott will work one-on-one with Heather to instruct her to count "one, two, three," take a pause, "four, five, six," etc. They will work together on this again at the end of the lesson when materials are collected to be put away. During the lesson, Heather will engage in class in several other ways, sometimes with Mrs. Prescott's guidance and other times with guidance from the algebra teacher or peers.

The Role of Paraeducators in Adapting

Some of our students with more significant disabilities have the support of a paraeducator at various times during their school day. Can Heather's paraeducator provide her specially designed instruction? Many state departments of education have issued guidelines on this question, including North Carolina. In their document, Public Schools of North Carolina: Educating the Whole Child, Considerations for Specially Designed Instruction (2019, p. 3), they answer the question *Who can provide specially designed instruction?*

- ◆ "Properly licensed special education teachers, including Birth-Kindergarten certified teachers, and related service providers with specialized training and competency in the area of need in collaboration with general education teachers."
- ◆ "General education teachers, therapy assistants and paraprofessionals, under the supervision of the special education teacher or related service provider, may *assist* in the provision of specially designed instruction, but may not be the primary provider of SDI."

The Indiana State Department of Education has similar guidelines (2018), but adds these additional caveats:

- ◆ "Adequate training is provided to the paraprofessional to support SDI."
- ◆ "On-going communication occurs between the paraprofessional and special education teacher or related service personnel."
- ◆ "A paraprofessional may not plan, deliver or lead initial instruction."

For Heather's paraeducator to support SDI, Mrs. Prescott will need to first try the instructional strategy with Heather. After a few sessions, Mrs. Prescott can have the paraeducator observe and then replicate the intervention. If Mrs. Prescott feels that the paraeducator is effectively implementing the strategy, the paraeducator can continue to provide the SDI, communicating with the teachers on a regular basis about Heather's progress. Mrs. Prescott should observe regularly, look at progress data and occasionally work with Heather directly on this goal. If she decides that the strategy is not working, she will take over the instructional lead again, redesigning her approach to the goal.

Similar to the art of rock balancing mentioned at the beginning of the chapter, adapting a lesson is a balancing act. The specialist must balance:

- ◆ The needs of an individual student
- ◆ The needs of the group of students
- ◆ The curriculum
- ◆ The teaching team
- ◆ A limited amount of time
- ◆ Available resources

A quick Google search yields hundreds of photos of balanced rocks and cairns. Some of these rock sculptures appear physically impossible, yet were feasible with patience and perseverance. Adapting lessons with SDI is also very feasible with enough patience and a growth mindset.

To Sum Up

- ◆ SDI can transform a lesson for just a few or for the whole class. By using multi-sensory input, visual supports, chunking and other research-based strategies, special education teachers and related professionals can adapt instruction so that students with disabilities are more successful.

◆ The special education teacher or related professional designs and delivers the adaptations, but other team members may help. The specialist should provide initial instruction, but can train others to continue the interventions, as long as they are communicating regularly about student progress. The specialist will want to observe and interact with the student frequently enough to be sure that the specially designed instruction is working.

Reflection Questions

◆ What can you do to stay current with evidence-based practices? How might you enhance this component of your own professional growth?
◆ In addition to students with IEPs, who else might benefit when you transform a lesson? Have you promoted this with your general education partners?

Try This

◆ Read a research article about an instructional practice. Brainstorm ways it might apply to your own teaching situation. If appropriate, weave it into a lesson you are designing for one of your students.
◆ Think of a student who has goals several years below others in a classroom and is working on alternate standards. Then brainstorm ideas for how to address their goals by using this perspective shift: *"Look at the lesson for ALL that it offers, not just its traditionally intended purpose."*

9

Planning Step 6: Attend to Access and Executive Function Skills

The overhead speakers crackle with a choppy gate announcement as I look for my flight on the departure board. Someone bumps my arm as they hurry past, dragging two wheelie suitcases behind them. I scan the board, but it refreshes every ten seconds, forcing me to begin my search all over again. Finally, I realize that I am right next to my gate and can grab a few minutes of rest before lining up. Every seat in the area has someone sitting in it except for one – covered with sandwich wrappings and loose French fries. Choosing to stand, I lean against the floor-to-ceiling glass windows and look out over the tarmac. Dozens of planes are in transition, pilots and mechanics are busy with their checks and baggage handlers are tossing suitcases. Off in the distance is the control tower – the visible symbol of airport management – but hidden in numerous other spaces are the people who keep it all running smoothly. I marvel at the coordination it takes to move people safely through the air and hope that today will be one of those problem-free days.

Experts at the Center on the Developing Child at Harvard University must also fly from time to time, for they have compared the process to executive functions. "Having executive function in the brain is like having an air traffic control system at a busy airport to manage the arrivals and departures

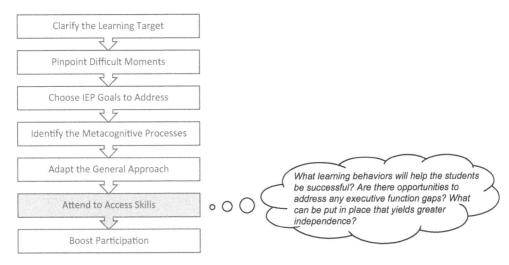

Figure 9.1 Planning Step 6

of dozens of planes on multiple runways" (2011). Add to air traffic all the other processes that need to be managed at an airport, and every person there is busy with executive functions. As we travel through an airport, we rely on our executive function, but we also use access skills to help us arrive at our destination (Figure 9.1).

Access Skills

The term *access skills* refers to those skills we need to access the curriculum, but which are not explicitly represented by the academic standards. In an airport this might include scanning a departure board for key information. In a classroom, access skills include things like raising your hand, taking turns and sitting up in your seat. Access skills can also include the missing pre-requisite academic skill that a student needs to be successful. For example, a student who is not a fluent reader will have a difficult time accessing a high school biology textbook. Reading fluency will not be specifically stated in the science standards for that grade level, but becomes a significant challenge for students who are missing it. Other examples of access skills include:

- ◆ Communication
- ◆ Problem solving
- ◆ Self-advocacy
- ◆ Gross and Fine Motor
- ◆ Inter/Intrapersonal

Figure 9.2 Relationship Between Access Skills and Executive Function

◆ Organization
◆ Technology
◆ Work Readiness

Access skills is a broad term that encompasses a subset of skills referred to as executive functions (see Figure 9.2).

Executive Function

Executive function is also an umbrella term and includes a set of cognitive processes that are used for successfully navigating a complex situation. The Center on the Developing Child has grouped these processes into three dimensions:

Working Memory – the capacity to hold and manipulate information in our head

Inhibitory Control – the capacity to master and filter our thoughts and actions

Cognitive Flexibility – the capacity to adjust to changing situations, demands or perspectives

Other experts break these down further into eleven categories (Dawson and Guare 2018) or more. The most common categories are shown in Table 9.1.

All of these executive functions are needed to be a successful student, yet they develop at various ages for students. We aren't born with these skills. Most of us are born with the *potential* for these skills, and their development is affected by our experiences from infancy through adolescence. Students with disabilities may be disadvantaged prior to birth due to a number of factors that can impair executive function in the brain. Therefore, it is imperative that specialists create strong plans for addressing these deficits so that their students will be able to succeed in school and beyond.

Table 9.1 Common Executive Function Categories

Category	Description
Planning	Look ahead, determine importance, map out how to reach a goal
Organization	Design and implement methods to keep track of information, materials, events, requirements
Time Management	Estimate and allocate time, prioritize use of time
Working Memory	Hold information and apply to current complex situations
Metacognition	Be aware of how one thinks, observe self, evaluate personal actions and processes
Response Inhibition	Think before you act, identify impact, delay gratification
Self-Regulation	Manage thoughts, emotions and actions, awareness of impact
Sustained Attention	Maintain attention for a long duration despite distractions
Task Initiation	Begin a task, avoid temptation to procrastinate
Flexibility	Adapt thoughts, emotions and actions in response to changing conditions, rethink, revise
Goal-Directed Persistence	Continue effort toward a goal, persevere despite obstacles or waning interest

Access Skills and Executive Function in Action

Imagine Mr. Harvey's eighth-grade language arts class with this agenda for the period.
AGENDA

◆ Bell Ringer – Five minutes journal writing – How does prejudice impact your life?
◆ Optional sharing and group discussion
◆ Next chapter *Dear Martin*
◆ Silent Gallery Splash and Analysis
◆ Homework/Assignments

What are the executive function or access skills that a student might need to successfully participate in this class?

If you identified all of the executive function categories and several access skills, you are right! Before ever arriving at class a student will need time management skills to pass quickly from his last class, planning and organization skills to bring the right materials with him and persistence to avoid all the temptations that exist in the halls. Upon entering class, he will need impulse control to seat himself quickly and quietly, remember to look at the board for the bell ringer and basic reading skills to know the task. The journal prompt requires metacognition, while the sharing will require interpersonal skills such as active listening and empathy. As they read the next chapter in their novel, the student's working memory will be utilized as he tries to make connections and comprehend the story sequence. During the Splash activity, students are expected to silently move from chart to chart on the walls, adding ideas and analyzing for patterns or differences. This will require many of the executive function skills, as well as an understanding of "clockwise" and "patterns," both taught in earlier grades. When the fire alarm unexpectedly goes off, the student will need flexibility and self-regulation during a fairly chaotic process.

Now imagine Nick, a student with autism spectrum disorder (ASD) in Mr. Harvey's class. Executive function deficits are one of the hallmarks of this condition. Nick is likely to have several needs in this area, some of which are represented by IEP goals and others that are not. Specially designed instruction will be necessary for Nick to develop the skills needed to navigate this class and the world around him. While he begins with deficits, the good news from neuroscientists is hopeful. "The same neuroplasticity that leaves executive functioning skills vulnerable to genetic and environmental disruption also presents the possibility of actively promoting the successful development of these skills" (Center on the Developing Child 2011, p. 8). This is the reason that Step 7 in the SDI Planning Process emphasizes access and executive function skills.

Mrs. Adele's fifth-grade class of twenty-eight includes three English language learners, six students with IEPs and two students with 504 plans. She also has two students who were tested for a potential disability, but did not qualify for services. Mrs. Adele has an inclusion mindset, believing that all students belong, no matter their circumstances, and that together they will figure it out. Below her signature block in all work emails is a quote from Steven Covey, "Strength lies in differences, not in similarities." Mrs. Adele is grateful to have a special educator and an English language specialist on her team who are both highly skilled in their domains. While she wishes these specialists spent more time in her classroom, she appreciates whatever time they spend co-planning and co-teaching.

Mrs. Adele and Mrs. Seay, the special education teacher, are efficiently moving through their planning tasks for the coming week.

MRS. ADELE: Have you noticed how much nagging we both seem to be doing so that students get their math work done? I am annoying myself with it all. I can only begin to imagine how annoying it is to the kids and it doesn't seem to be helping.

MRS. SEAY: Yup. I feel like a countdown clock. "10 minutes left. Only 5 minutes left." Personally, I know that I don't respond well to nagging. It sometimes makes me dig my heels in further.

MRS. ADELE: Next week's math plans call for a lot of independent work projects. Can you think of a different way to handle it?

MRS. SEAY: I'd be happy to mull it over. Actually, Tonia and Kareem both have IEP goals related to time management, work completion and sustained attention. This will fit right in with those.

MRS. ADELE: Great, but we have lots of other students who might need instruction about this. Can you lead a lesson for the whole class?

MRS. SEAY: Sure. Let me think about it and create something for Monday.

Mrs. Seay allows the challenge to percolate for a day. As it does, she considers her own metacognitive process for managing time. She thinks about Tonia and Kareem's unique learning profiles, wanting to use their strengths to build their capacity with efficient task completion. Previous formative assessments make her confident that the issue is not an academic deficit in math, but instead an executive function issue. She creates a micro-lesson on planning time allocation for a task with clock strips (Figure 9.3).

On Monday, Mrs. Seay gives every student a clock strip and asks them to fill in the start clock to show 10:00. She explains that they will have twenty minutes to work on the day's math project and has students figure out what time they should be finished, marking it on their clocks. Finally, they figure out the half-way point, 10:10. Mrs. Adele then hands out a project worksheet and explains the task. Mrs. Seay jumps in and asks students to analyze the task to determine where they should be at the half-way point. The teachers encourage a bit of debating, asking students to explain their opinions. Mrs. Seay points out tips for estimating the time needed. When they reach a class agreement, Mrs. Seay directs students to label the half-way point on their worksheets. Mrs. Adele circulates, checking in on Tonia, Kareem and others.

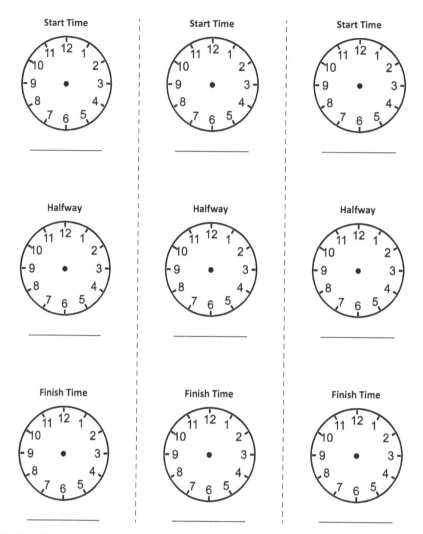

Figure 9.3 Clock Strips

Once the project begins, Mrs. Seay and Mrs. Adele replace their frequent nagging with only a few, more subtle prompts of "check the clock." Near the end of the lesson, they lead a discussion with the class about this time management strategy, asking them to reflect on their personal experience with it. The teachers decide to use it several more times before teaching students how to mark time in their work without the use of the clock strips. Mrs. Seay will provide select students with more intensive practice through small-group instruction at convenient times throughout the coming month.

In this example, it is the instruction on time management that qualifies as SDI, not the paper clock strip. The strips are tools, or accommodations, similar to providing a highlighter, a graphic organizer or a picture schedule. *Instruction*, the very important third word in SDI, is what leads to learning and independence. However, students may also need accommodations to assist with missing access or executive function skills. Calculators, spell check, color-coding, reminder cards, quiet spots – these are all tools that students with or without IEPs might benefit from in any classroom setting. The role of the specialist is to ensure that students with disabilities are receiving the right combination of both accommodations and SDI so that they can successfully access the general education curriculum and meet the standards.

The vast majority of students with IEPs have intelligence that falls within what we think of as the average range. This indicates that they should be able to manage the academic difficulty of the general education curriculum, except for other issues that get in the way. Just as the vast majority of us can navigate an airport for a vacation trip, some miss their flights due to oversleeping, an overly optimistic prediction of drive time to the airport, forgetting to bring required identification or one too many drinks in the airport bar!

The mantra proposed in Chapter 8 may help educators as they try to identify the missing access skills needed to be successful in a lesson. *"Look at the lesson for ALL that it offers, not just it's traditionally intended purpose."* If we change just one word, "offers," to the word "requires," we can consider the demands placed on the student that fall outside of the grade level academic standards. This is where so many of our students get tripped up on their journey.

Speech/Language Pathologists (SLPs) often work on skills that fall under the heading of access or executive function. Kristin Hutchins, an elementary school SLP, uses video to provide SDI on social and communication goals. She writes "Using videos are one of my (and definitely my students') favorite ways of observing and identifying social thinking concepts" (2018). Hutchins shares an example of how to use episodes of *Mr. Bean*, a British sitcom, in which the lead character is rather unaware of many of the social norms and is baffled by everyday activities. The video clips are minimally verbal with lots of exaggerated facial expressions, providing myriad opportunities for students to practice reading nonverbal cues.

Hutchins suggests this sequence:

1 Show a brief video clip of Mr. Bean in a socially awkward scene.
2 Pause the video occasionally and ask students to make smart guesses about Mr. Bean's emotions.

3   Place sticky note thought bubbles directly on the screen to capture possible thoughts behind Mr. Bean's expressions.
4   Have students make a list of expected and unexpected social rules that apply to the scene.
5   Ask students to reflect on their own feelings. Did the scene make them feel awkward or uncomfortable? What would they have done?

Using video as a social skills teaching tool is a high-leverage practice with peer-reviewed research to support it. As a starting point, it allows students to see others' behavior as a model and compare it to their own. When paired with practice in multiple settings, timely feedback and self-reflection, video can be utilized very effectively for students with a range of disabilities. Hutchins' use of video in this example is special, addresses unique needs and will lead to generalization – all characteristics of SDI.

Self-monitoring is another research-based strategy that helps students to become more aware of their own behaviors. Awareness is almost always a prerequisite step to behavior change. Some students with disabilities have relatively minor behavioral changes to make, while others contend with a major behavior disorder. In either case, explicit instruction in self-monitoring can have a positive impact on targeted behaviors. In addition, explicit instruction in executive functioning has been shown to have positive influences on early literacy and math skills (McClelland et al. 2007). Logically, this makes sense. If a student's executive function deficits are interfering with academic learning, we can extrapolate and safely assume that they are also negatively impacting other content areas such as science.

Mr. Hartman, a veteran teacher with a love for all things science related, embedded lots of experiments into his science lessons. Each of these experiments came with critical, multi-step directions. He noticed early on in the school year that Isaac, a student with an ADHD diagnosis, appeared to be tuning out during directions. Unfortunately, Mr. Hartman didn't have a co-teacher or a paraeducator in the class, as they were typically assigned to the math and language arts periods. He sent a text message to Isaac's case manager and asked to meet with her. Mrs. Buchanan was providing service to Isaac in two co-taught periods, but was happy to consult with Mr. Hartman.

Mr. Hartman explained his concern about Isaac's attention. Knowing that the science teacher loved strategies with an evidence base, Mrs. Buchanan suggested a self-monitoring strategy and promised to send him an article or two. She also offered to drop in to the class to provide a lesson on self-monitoring to all of the students. She described her idea:

MRS. BUCHANAN: I'll cut graph paper up into small pieces, with a 15 x 15 grid. We will have students label the X axis as dates spanning the next two weeks. Along the Y access they can choose from a list of behaviors that they want to self-monitor, such as attention, hand raising, volunteering or having their materials.

MR. HARTMAN: Maybe at that point I could make the connection to the data collection we do during our experiments.

MRS. BUCHANAN: That's a great idea. I think it might be best if I pre-teach this strategy to Isaac. I'll see if he can come see me for a few minutes before school begins. If not, I'll find a few minutes during one of the co-taught classes I have him in. I'll explain to the class that throughout the lesson they will hear a random beep. When it occurs, we will all pause and ask ourselves 'Am I paying attention?' 'Did I raise my hand?' or whatever your goal is. I'll emphasize that there will be no negative consequences – this usually decreases dishonesty.

MR. HARTMAN: So, the first time is really to collect baseline data?

MRS. BUCHANAN: Yes, the first couple of days probably. Then you can have students use highlighters to indicate a goal line on their graph. Each day they continue to gather data and note it on their graph.

MR. HARTMAN: That sounds simple enough. Anything else I need to know to keep it going?

MRS. BUCHANAN: Just make sure each day has the same number of self-monitoring beeps so that they can compare their growth. I can't be here every day, but I will arrange to be back on the fourth day, especially to check in on Isaac.

In this example, the special education teacher is developing the SDI, initiating it, modeling it for the general education teacher, and monitoring its effectiveness. In addition to supporting Isaac, her collaboration has created professional growth for the general education teacher, who now has one more tool in his bucket.

Special educators also bring value to the classroom with their knowledge of memory research and related strategies. Because so many students receiving special education experience deficits in working memory, specialists tend to seek out and gather information in this arena. While general education teachers can also find this information, their curriculum content needs often take priority. It makes sense in collaborative relationships to capitalize on the unique expertise that both bring, rather than trying to become clones of each other.

Philosopher Friedrich Nietzsche famously said, "The advantage of a bad memory is that one enjoys several times the same good things for the first time." While this tongue-in-cheek comment might apply to a five-star restaurant or a beautiful beach, a poor memory is truly a disadvantage in school settings. Education researchers, cognitive scientists and neuroscientists have published thousands of studies, articles, blogs and books on this topic. An excellent example of this is www.retrievalpractice.org, a hub of research and resources on the process of retrieving information when it is needed. Educators typically focus on getting information into students' heads through lecture, activities, re-reading and review of notes. These methods can work to develop short-term learning but don't guarantee we'll remember it. Retrieval practice is the process of actively, intentionally bringing information to mind and examining what we know. Research shows that retrieval practice dramatically improves long-term memory (Agarwal et al. 2017).

Mrs. Arsenau, a middle-school special education teacher, participated in a district-wide book club last year. All of the members agreed to read *Make it Stick* by Peter Brown and colleagues during the first semester, and Marilee Sprenger's *How to Teach So Students Remember* the second semester. This year, she is building retrieval practice into her instruction as often as possible, especially for Abby and Martin, two students with memory deficits. She began by engaging students in a discussion about retrieval in everyday life. She then shared with them that science shows retrieval practice is more effective than review. Mrs. Arsenau had them practice by writing down everything they could remember from their conversation so far. This helped the students to see that retrieval wasn't complicated – it was simple! Mrs. Arsenau suggested that they create Pause and Retrieve Sticky Notes to insert into their social studies textbook at the bottom of each page. When they encountered one, it would serve as a reminder to grab a piece of paper and write down everything they could remember, without looking back at the information. (For digital texts, students can place the sticky note at the bottom of their screen or set a timer.)

> Improved memory has a domino effect that initiates a succession of many positive outcomes.

Over the next several weeks, Mrs. Arsenau checked in with Abby and Martin to reflect on how the strategy was working for them. Once they had both developed the habit, Mrs. Arsenau suggested they try using it in another class of their choice. Where did they need the most memory help? Which class lent itself best to the strategy? Both students reflected and made choices, taking ownership for applying the strategy. As their retrieval improved, so did their quiz scores and confidence levels. Improved memory has a domino effect that initiates a succession of many positive outcomes.

Planning Checklist

Specialists also need great memories in order to effectively and completely fulfill the requirements of their day-to-day work. Cognitive overload can be avoided by distinguishing between what you need to remember and what can be accessed as a resource. When you want to work smarter and faster, a simple checklist can make a big difference. There's no need to try to remember all of the executive function and access skill categories. Instead, keep a copy of the following checklist with your lesson planner and simply glance over it when you are designing your instruction for the week (Table 9.2). Ask yourself:

◆ Does the lesson require any of the following skills?
◆ Do we have students that have deficits in one or more categories?
◆ Do we have IEP goals or accommodations in any of these areas?
◆ Which will be the most important ones to focus on so that the student can participate successfully?

Caution

With the best of intentions, adults that work with students with disabilities often help their charges too much. The term "Velcro phenomenon" refers to adults who have a tendency to stick to the side of the student more often than is necessary. This phenomenon occurs quite regularly when paraeducators are assigned as a one-on-one support for a particular student. They can develop very strong relationships – mostly a good thing – but can get in the way of emerging independence. Experts at the Center on the Developing Child remind us, "Environments that foster executive functioning are characterized by adult-child relationships that guide children from complete dependence on adult support to gradual assumption of the 'executive" role for themselves. Such environments neither expect children to have more advanced skills than are reasonable for their age, *nor do they treat them as if they had no executive capabilities*" (emphasis added) (2011, p. 6).

One of the job responsibilities of a special education teacher is to guide paraeducators in understanding how to fade their assistance over time so that students build independent skills. It may be as simple as helping paraeducators recognize that a student doesn't need to learn how to wait for help from a teacher if the paraeducator is always at their side. Stepping away from the assigned student to circulate the room might actually be a way to prioritize the student's need to figure things out more independently. One-on-one assignments should never be interpreted as "at their side at every moment" unless specifically required to avoid danger to the student or others.

Table 9.2 Planning for Access and Executive Function Skills

Access or Executive Function Category	Required for lesson ✓	First names of students with related deficits	First names of students with related IEP goals	First names of students with related accommodations	Starred priorities ★
Communication					
Problem solving					
Goal-Directed Persistence					
Self-Advocacy					
Gross and Fine Motor					
Inter/Intrapersonal					
Planning					
Organization					
Technology					
Work Readiness					
Time Management					
Working Memory					
Metacognition					
Self-Regulation					
Response Inhibition					
Sustained Attention					
Task Initiation					
Flexibility					

Similarly, a special education teacher who works one-on-one with a student to complete a worksheet, must be cautious about offering too much assistance. With the best of intentions, we can diminish their opportunities to assume these executive function roles for themselves.

Just as most of us feel a sense of accomplishment when we navigate a new airport successfully, especially in a foreign country, our students with disabilities also want and need the experience of a productive struggle that leads to success. As artist Michael John Bobak reminds us, "All progress takes place outside the comfort zone."

To Sum Up

◆ A hallmark of many disabilities is a deficit in access or executive function skills. These vital skills cut across all content disciplines and grade levels, having an enormous impact on school success.

◆ Many students will have IEP goals that directly address access or executive function skills. In these cases, specially designed instruction will be necessary. At other times, a variety of accommodations will be helpful to students with deficits. When SDI is involved, it should be based on evidence from peer-reviewed research whenever possible.

Reflection Questions

◆ What category of executive function skills do you know the best? Which do you understand the least? How might you improve your knowledge in that area so as to best serve your students?

◆ Do you shine a light on your unique expertise in executive function and share it with colleagues so that everyone can grow in their professional skills? How might you do this more proactively?

Try This

◆ Choose one executive function and do an internet search. Pick an article from a respected website and read it without taking notes. Employ retrieval practice by pausing at the end and writing down everything you can remember.

◆ Ask colleagues if they are interested in starting a professional book club about executive function skills. Research a few titles to propose.

10

Planning Step 7:
Boost Participation

Imagine that your school district has recently embraced restorative practices as a conflict resolution approach to reduce bullying and violence. Part of the roll-out plan requires every staff person in the district to participate in a full day of in-person professional development on the topic. You arrive in the parking lot with a few minutes to spare and walk into the auditorium along with several of your colleagues. The back rows have been taped off so that everyone will sit closer to the front, but there are still plenty of seats available throughout the audience. You spot a friend and grab a seat next to them, pulling your laptop out of your bag. The expert in restorative practices is introduced, shares her first slide and begins the training session.

During the next six hours, which of the following do you experience?

- Wandering attention
- Misunderstanding of material
- Falling behind in notetaking
- Talking off-topic with a friend
- Avoiding becoming a volunteer
- Feeling perturbed at having to do an activity
- Checking email
- Shopping online
- Grading papers

- Sending texts
- Drooping eyelids or grumbling stomach
- Feeling frustrated about the lack of relevance

Now imagine that you have experienced several years of failure in school, have a learning disability and low expectations of yourself. Would your participation level drop even further?

Why Participation Matters

While many variables affect participation and engagement, there is one constant – when it drops, so does learning. Teachers can spend hours creating a lesson or project, but if it doesn't engage the student, the time was wasted. With time being a precious commodity, teachers will want to attend to what the research says about boosting engagement and participation. Indirectly, this issue has been addressed in each of the first six SDI Planning Steps, but Step 7, Boost Participation, provides us with the directive to be intentional and unambiguous in our design (Figure 10.1).

> While many variables affect participation and engagement, there is one constant – when it drops, so does learning.

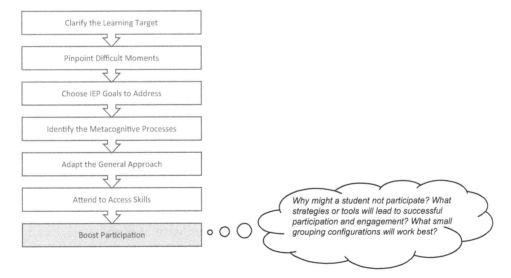

Figure 10.1 Planning Step 7

Essential Terms

Dictionaries provides us with two main definitions for *participation*:

1 the action of taking part in something
2 an association with others in a relationship with specified rights and obligations

At a minimum, we want our students with disabilities taking part in our lessons, as the first definition describes. However, most teachers want more than this! A student who sees themselves as being in a relationship with the teacher and their peers, with certain rights and obligations as part of the learning process will be engaged to a deeper level. A teacher who recognizes the rights of all to participate will intentionally design instruction that is accessible and equitable.

Phillip Schlechty, educator and school improvement advocate, tells us that a student is engaged when they are attentive, committed, persistent and find meaning and value in the work. He warns, "sometimes on-task behavior is confused with engagement. On-task behavior indicates only that a student is attentive to a task. It says nothing of the student's willingness to persist with the task when he or she experiences difficulty. It also says nothing about the value the student attaches to the task or the meaning he or she associates with activity related to it" (2011, p. 14).

Schlechty went on to identify five possible responses that a student might have to a learning task:

1 Engagement
2 Strategic compliance
3 Ritual compliance
4 Retreatism
5 Rebellion

Of course, rebellion and retreatism are clearly unacceptable to anyone who cares about children. But what about compliance? Teachers generally prefer compliant students – those who don't disrupt the learning process. However, students who are ritually compliant are doing the bare minimum, thinking to themselves "What do I have to do to be done and get out?" These students will learn at very low levels. Again, this is unacceptable to those who care.

Students who are strategically compliant can learn at high levels, but are unlikely to have a depth of understanding or retain the information. Extrinsic rewards such as grades, praise or college admission are the motivation for these students, rather than the learning itself. Many of these students are seen as successful, causing teachers to feel satisfied with their teaching practices. Special educators are often thrilled to guide children with disabilities into becoming students who fit this description. But what if we can do even more?

The engaged student is personally invested in the work, finding it interesting and meaningful enough that they will persist through difficulties. Students with disabilities frequently encounter difficult moments on their learning journey, so persistence is an essential quality for success. Sustained, vibrant engagement is the overarching goal of Step 7 in our process.

What Does the Research Say?

Thousands of research studies have explored the variables involved in student engagement. Researchers Robert Marzano and Debra Pickering performed a meta-analysis of the research, looking for patterns that might guide educators (2010). They identified four major categories that lead to student engagement – emotion, interest, importance and efficacy. As teachers plan and reflect, certain questions can lead us to boost engagement in each area (Table 10.1).

Robyn Jackson, an expert in educational equity, believes that the seed of participation is student choice. In her book, *How to Motivate Reluctant Learners*, Jackson writes, "Our students' decision to invest in the classroom is directly related to whether or not they have the currency our assignments, activities and broader academic and behavioral expectations are asking for – and whether or not they believe that currency will help them achieve a desired outcome or meet a particular need" (2011, p. 15). Her statement shows a clear intersection with Marzano and Pickering's thoughts about student interest, importance and efficacy. Jackson's advice to teachers – "Make learning feel so safe and look so attractive that all students will want to lower their resistance, shed their armor, and take the risk to learn in your classroom" (18). For students who struggle, whatever the reason, we want our classroom culture to be compassionate and safe, while still challenging enough to prevent boredom and yield significant learning.

Jackson recommends teachers consider the SMORES criteria (Table 10.2), when asking students to invest in their learning, especially students who are already caught up in a cycle of failure. An examination of these six criteria show that they are clearly applicable to students with disabilities and our planning process for SDI. For example, Jackson's third criteria, "The investment should be stated in terms of its observable behaviors," supports the need to write a clear learning target for the lesson in student friendly terms. Her sixth criteria, "The investment behavior should not be something students will perceive as overwhelming," reminds us to adapt instruction so that it is at just the right level for student success.

Table 10.1 Engagement Boosters

Engagement Booster	Reflective Questions
Emotion	• How will the student feel during this lesson? • Do students feel accepted in the classroom? • Does the lesson use emotion in a positive way to engage? • How might tension, debate, storytelling and celebration be added? • How might relationships with peers or adults be impacting learning? • Does the classroom environment feel safe for risk-taking? • How do I monitor my own demeanor during a lesson?
Interest	• Does this tap into student interest? • Have I built in choices for students? • Do students have an opportunity to move? • Is the learning task game-like or fun? • Have I used novelty to grab attention? • How can I use questioning techniques to pique interest? • How will the pacing of the lesson impact interest?
Importance	• Have I conveyed the importance of the learning target? • Do students see this as important? • How have I made this relevant to students' lives? • Is there a way to tap into pop culture or contemporary issues? • Have I helped students see connections to other important things? • Is there a way to make this more authentic? • Have I tapped into intrinsic motivation rather than extrinsic?
Efficacy	• Does the student feel they can accomplish the task? • Does the student have a fixed or a growth mindset? • What successful role models could be mentioned in association with this lesson? • Have I built in scaffolding and supports? • Can chunking be utilized to make students feel more efficacious? • How are students reflecting and monitoring their growth? • Does the lesson utilize student strengths?

Table 10.2 The SMORES Criteria for Shaping the Right Kind of Investment

Specific	The investment should consist of specific steps rather than a vague request.
Meaningful	The investment should help students use the currencies they have to get something they want or meet a basic need.
Observable	The investment should be stated in terms of its observable behaviors.
Realistic	The investment should be at the top of students' "reach" given their present currencies.
Worth the Effort	The investment should lead to immediate and short-term payoffs.
Small	The investment behavior should not be something students will perceive as overwhelming.

Republished with permission of Mindsteps, Inc., from Robyn Jackson, *How to Motivate Reluctant Learners*, 2011; permission conveyed through Copyright Clearance Center, Inc.

John Hattie, another esteemed researcher in the field of education, has examined several thousand studies to identify exactly which practices have yielded significant learning for students. Hattie pinpoints practices that have the "potential to considerably accelerate" as having an effect size of > 4.0. These can be considered influences that have the potential to bring about more than a year's growth in a year's time – something many students with disabilities need. Table 10.3 shows some of the influences over which teachers have control.

Some of these teacher practices have an indirect impact on engagement while others are much more directly connected. For example, if a student has poor study skills and performs badly on quizzes and tests, they are likely to lose confidence, get frustrated and disengage. Or if a student struggles with academic vocabulary, they will fall behind in comprehension and perhaps begin to retreat from the learning. Hattie concluded that there is little instruction for students on how to learn. "At present, strategy teaching is notable by its absence" (2012, p. 126). Specialists will want to have solid strategies in all nine areas. Many strategies have already been explored in earlier chapters and can also be found represented in the lesson examples in Appendix A.

Two influences that bear direct impact on participation are classroom discussion and small-group instruction. These influences deserve thoughtful consideration during this step of the SDI planning process.

Table 10.3 Selected Factors that Influence Student Achievement

Influence	Effect Size
Study Skills	.45
Practice Testing	.46
Small-Group Instruction	.47
Notetaking	.51
Imagery	.51
Modality Effect	.55
Tactile Stimulation	.58
Self-Verbalization and Self-Questioning	.59
Vocabulary Instruction	.63
Rehearsal and Memorization	.73
Summarizing	.74
Reciprocal Teaching	.74
Self-judgement and Reflection	.75
Planning and Prediction	.75
Elaboration and Organization	.75
Teacher Clarity	.76
Mnemonics	.80
Classroom Discussion	.82
Transfer Strategies	.86
Success Criteria	.88
Integrating Prior Knowledge	.93
Teacher Estimates of Achievement	1.44

2020 http://www.visiblelearningmetax.com/

Classroom Discussion

Picture a recent lesson that you taught or observed. Who was doing most of the talking? Lessons that include an abundance of student talk increase achievement *if* the conversation is accessible and equitable. Many teachers have begun to increase student talk and they should be applauded for their efforts. However, if teachers have a limited number of discussion protocols, students with disabilities may be left behind. Simple "turn and talk" strategies may not be accessible and equitable for several reasons, including:

- Auditory processing deficits
- Inadequate processing or think time
- Poor working memory
- Wandering attention
- Anxiety or shyness
- Speech and language deficits
- Partially known or unknown vocabulary
- Lack of confidence
- Unclear expectations

In addition, "turn and talk" usually does not lead to what Zaretta Hammond calls "cognitive chewing" (2020, p. 45). Cognitive chewing facilitates deep thinking, leading to deeper, richer conversations. Student with disabilities may need accommodations such as extended wait time in order to experience cognitive chewing, or they may need specially designed instruction in specific skills such as listening. Classroom teachers can use a variety of discussion protocols – procedures that allow everyone time to think, talk and listen – to ensure that all students participate in meaningful ways. Many educators have shared ideas for sparking deep discussion, including Jennifer Gonzalez' *Big List of Class Discussion Strategies* (https://www.cultofpedagogy.com/speaking-listening-techniques/) and the School Reform Initiatives' list of protocols (https://www.schoolreforminitiative.org/protocols/). Specialists may need to adapt these protocols to meet individual student needs.

Boosting Participation in Action

Mr. Stahl uses a fishbowl protocol in his classroom to engage all students in responding to text. Four students sit in the center of the room, while remaining students gather around the edge of the circle to observe and take notes as the students discuss a passage. At a point decided by Mr. Stahl, four students from the outer circle move in and each taps a student to change places. While this strategy has worked successfully for him in the past, he now has a number of students with language deficits and wants to be sure they can participate successfully.

Ms. Tangara, a new speech language pathologist, is bursting with ideas from her college classes and is excited to collaborate with the general education teachers in the building. She doesn't have time in her schedule to co-teach with Mr. Stahl regularly, but can co-plan and co-teach a few lessons each month. Discussion protocols were a part of her pre-service training and so Ms. Tangara has some suggestions for how to adapt the plan.

MS. TANGARA: We have two students in this class that have similar IEP goals to each other – the student will be able to maintain a topic of conversation for at least 3 reciprocal turns. Do you have any other students that struggle with staying on topic after their first response?

MR. STAHL: A few, although I want the conversation to be authentic enough that students can make personal connections without feeling too much rigidity.

MS. TANGARA: Got you. What if we have all students spend a few minutes in groups of four before we begin the fishbowl? We can give each group a large piece of paper and have each student do a quick graffiti brain dump on their area of the paper in response to the discussion prompt. After about a minute, we can direct them to look at what each other wrote and draw lines, arrows, stars, etc. showing connections they notice or aha's. Then, when they meet inside the fishbowl, they can have their group's graffiti in the middle as a reminder of some ways to add or piggyback on other's comments.

MR. STAHL: I like it. But is that enough instruction for you to feel that you've provided your SDI?

MS. TANGARA: Well, I'd like a few minutes of class time to explicitly point out to students the value of carrying notes with you into conversations. I know I always have a cheat sheet of notes when I go into meetings. Do you?

MR. STAHL: Sure. Perhaps we could both show them an authentic example under the document camera?

MS. TANGARA: Great idea! And then I might work with just a small group during our next co-taught lesson to reinforce this strategy and work on generalization.

Ms. Tangara's adaptation reduces working memory load, increases processing time, supports language needs and improves student confidence, with almost no prep for either teacher! With her specialist's perspective, she was able to transform the general education practice so that all students in the class could be involved.

Wait Time

In order for students to participate fluently in classroom discussions, practicing predictable routines or protocols is essential. Frequent changes to process will make it much more difficult for students with disabilities to feel comfortable and confident. In addition, conversation that requires an immediate response will not allow students enough processing time. In education circles, this is often referred to as "wait time" – the time between a teacher's question and when the first student is called upon to answer.

In 1986, Mary Budd Rowe reviewed the literature on wait time and found some astonishing outcomes. When teachers waited a minimum of three seconds before allowing a response, ten positive outcomes occurred:

1 The length of responses increased between 300% and 700%.
2 More inferences were supported by evidence and logical argument.
3 The incidence of speculative thinking increased.
4 The number of questions asked by students increased.
5 Student–student exchanges increased; teacher-centered "show and tell" behavior decreased.
6 Failures to respond decreased.
7 Disciplinary moves by teachers decreased.
8 The variety of students participating voluntarily increased.
9 Student confidence, as reflected in fewer inflected responses, increased.
10 Achievement improved on written measures that were cognitively complex.

Rowe also identified a second wait time – what she called letting the student's answer "hang in the air." Most teachers quickly provide feedback to an answer ("Yes!") and move on to the next question. Rowe found that if a teacher pauses for a few seconds after the student answers, all of the students may benefit. The answering student might expand their initial statement, while other students might be comparing their answer to the one given, evaluating whether it will be deemed correct and thinking about what they might add to the conversation.

Some students with disabilities will need more than the minimum three seconds of wait time in order to participate. Special education researchers recommend 5-, 10-, and even 15-second intervals to allow students with disabilities to process the information and formulate a response (Johnson and Parker 2013). A word of caution, however, as research has shown that overly extended wait times can lead to diminishing positive results.

Is wait time an example of specially designed instruction? When we consider the guiding questions for SDI posed in Chapter 3, we conclude that it is an accommodation rather than SDI. Nonetheless, wait time will make other instruction accessible for students and is a staple ingredient of any effective class discussion or lesson.

Small-Group Instruction

Virtual meetings became a daily practice for most people in the world during the COVID-19 pandemic. No matter the platform, everyone was gathering in groups for work projects, family meals or happy hours with friends. The "Brady Bunch" effect of seeing a grid with small faces displayed side-by-side became a part of many nightly dreams and daytime memes. Once the group size grew larger than about a dozen, some of the images rolled over to a second or third or fourth screen to accommodate everyone. Zoom, one of the most popular platforms, automatically defaulted to placing meeting participants who did not turn on their video feed to the last screen.

While facilitating virtual workshops for educators during this time, I experienced a strong temptation to interact only with those who had their video feed on. The visual feedback was comforting, staying on the first screen was efficient for me, and letting adults determine their own level of participation seemed respectful. Most participants engaged in the chat box or other opportunities to respond, but I noticed the greatest increase in engagement when I sent everyone into small breakout rooms for discussion or application activities. Once the group size dropped from forty to four, or from two hundred to five, everyone participated.

Small-group instruction, whether for adults or for children, in virtual or in-person settings, has many benefits, including:

- The ability to develop a stronger relationship between teacher and student.
- Opportunities for up-close formative assessment and progress monitoring.
- Reduced anxiety for those who are shy or are embarrassed about deficits.
- Increased focus on the task through teacher prompting and distraction reduction.
- Opportunities for clarification and restating of directions.
- Instruction that is leveled to the readiness of a few, rather than the average of a large group.
- Interest-based lessons or examples.
- Strategy selection that is individualized by learner need.
- Increased opportunities to respond, as fewer group members can dominate.
- Teacher proximity to reduce inappropriate behavior while increasing success.

With so many benefits, and Hattie's meta-analysis showing the value, small-group instruction must be a component of inclusive instruction. Although SDI can be offered to individual students through whole-group lessons, it will be almost impossible to provide enough individualization and intensity to meet IEP goals without using some small-group instruction. Students with disabilities will retreat to the metaphorical fourth Zoom screen, video feed off and unengaged. Yet students with disabilities should not receive all of their instruction in small groups as this would diminish several benefits of inclusion. Finding the right balance will be a collaborative effort requiring a bit of trial and error and a plentitude of flexibility.

Teachers can improve the efficiency of decisions about small grouping practices by creating an anchor chart of their favorite configurations as in Figure 10.2 With the potential for dozens of grouping practices, narrowing your choices down to a manageable number is smart. By identifying a few configurations as favorites, colleagues can quickly and intentionally choose which will be most effective given the learning target and IEP goals of the day.

> Finding the right balance will be a collaborative effort requiring a bit of trial and error and a plentitude of flexibility.

As in so many of the SDI Planning Steps, intentionality is key. Guiding questions such as the following can aid in the decision-making process (Beninghof 2020, pp. 163–164).

◆ What is the purpose of the lesson?
◆ Are students expected to show mastery at the end of this lesson? If so, do we need intense, focused, small-group instruction to accomplish that?
◆ Does the lesson allow for lots of individual work time naturally? Will we be able to circulate and support individual students working at their own levels?
◆ Does the lesson allow for students to work with peers? Do we want to embed and encourage peer learning for this lesson?
◆ Is it possible to build in enough rigor and enrichment for students who are ready for more?
◆ Will we be able to balance participation opportunities in mixed-readiness groups?
◆ Can we design a whole-group lesson that includes strategies for simplifying the complexity while simultaneously including strategies for increasing the complexity?

Configuration 1 – Invitation Station

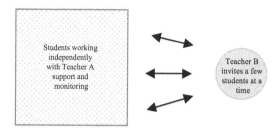

Configuration 2 – Pre-Teach/Re-Teach

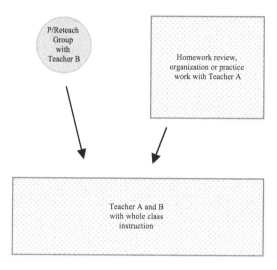

Configuration 3 – Double Time

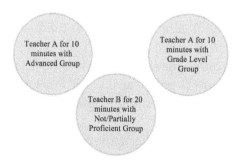

Figure 10.2 Sample Anchor Chart of Preferred Models for Small-Group Instruction

- ◆ Do we want students to be exposed to a variety of models, perspectives and ideas that might be more likely in a mixed-readiness group?
- ◆ Have we committed to any individualized objectives that can only be addressed in a smaller group setting?
- ◆ Will any students be embarrassed or anxious about working on this skill with peers who are more successful? Or will they be embarrassed about being readiness grouped?

Boosting Participation for Students on Alternate Standards

Mrs. Applegate, an elementary special education teacher, is meeting with her partner, Mrs. Patel, a first-grade teacher. Both are comfortable with and committed to small-group instruction. Listen in as they discuss a lesson that will allow Mrs. Applegate to provide SDI for Quinton, a student on alternate standards.

MRS. PATEL: I have a great idea for a writing lesson this week that will focus on adding details. I've got some thoughts about how to adapt it for Jeremiah and Anjou, but I'm not sure how we will include Quinton.

MRS. APPLEGATE: Quinton has two IEP goals we can integrate. One goal is for him to point to pictures in response to questions. We could have him do this with an online picture, and then have him click images to drop into a document for his writing. If we have a group working on iPads, he could join that group. He also has a goal to write his first name, so I'd love to do try some backward chaining to teach him the capital Q. He could do that with any students that are doing handwritten work.

MRS. PATEL: What if we set up several writing stations that children can go to depending on their needs? That way you could focus in more directly on his IEP goals. You and I could stay primarily at the iPad and handwriting stations, while students at a planning station can work independently with some resources. Tell me more about backward chaining. Is it something that other students might benefit from?

MRS. APPLEGATE: Absolutely! The idea is simple. Chaining involves analyzing a task and then teaching each step to create a chain of behaviors. You already do this when you are teaching letter and number formation. I learned about backward chaining in grad school. Backward chaining is used when the last step of the task is most important, as in the tail of the Q. So, I will give him the oval, and work with him on adding the tail. Once he has mastered the last step, we will move backwards in the chain so that eventually he will put the whole thing together.

MRS. PATEL: Could you try backward chaining with Amerika on her k? It still looks mostly like an l. We can place her in the same group with Quinton, and then perhaps a few other students who are writing independently.

MRS. APPLEGATE: Sounds good. So, we've agreed to make the three groups mixed-readiness, but intentionally place Quinton and Amerika together. I'll work with their handwriting group and rotate over to the iPad station with them, too. Are you comfortable with getting both the iPad and planning stations up and running?

By using small-group instruction, these teachers can more successfully address individual learning levels, monitor work and interact with students. Specially designed instruction can be offered to students like Quinton who are working on alternate standards or goals that differ significantly from their peers, while still being included in the activities of the class.

To Sum Up

◆ Participation and engagement are foundational to all learning. While students may not be outwardly rebellious or retreating, ritual or strategic compliance are less than ideal. Research shows that engagement and learning can be boosted in many ways, including classroom discussion and small-group instruction.

◆ Specially designed instruction can be provided within whole-group lessons but is much easier and more likely to happen in small groups. Within smaller groups, the specialist has the opportunity to level instruction based on IEP goals, connect with individual students, promote equitable discussion, provide corrective feedback and track progress. Effective teachers intentionally choose readiness-based or mixed-readiness grouping, depending on the learning target and the goals.

Reflection Questions

◆ Who is doing most of the talking in your classroom? What strategies or protocols might you use to boost student participation and guarantee equity?

◆ How many seconds do you wait after asking a question or providing a prompt? Do you have some students who frequently respond and others that do not? How can you remind yourself to extend the wait time so that more students are ready to answer? How might you help other team members – paraeducators, co-teachers, etc. – remember to allow enough wait time?

Try This

- ◆ Explore various discussion protocols. Which might help your students with disabilities have better access to classroom discussions? Are there any prerequisite skills that would need to be taught first? Any scaffolding that could form an entry step into richer conversation skills? Try a new discussion protocol and reflect on its effectiveness.
- ◆ Create a small-group anchor chart with three or four of your favorite small-group configurations. If you are collaborating with a partner to provide instruction, work on it together. Keep a copy of it with your planning materials for easy reference.

Part III

Fulfilling the Promise of SDI

Our promises to students were made with good intentions and must now be fulfilled with intentional actions. With a solid plan in place, it is time to implement with flexible devotion – devotion to the outcome and flexibility for the unexpected things that will pop up along the way. As with most complex endeavors, it is inevitable that instruction may not go exactly as planned. One component of the lesson may take longer than expected. A student's question might lead you in a different direction. Your mid-lesson formative assessment might indicate a need for more teacher modeling. Or the principal might decide that it's the perfect weather for a fire drill! Effective implementation and assessment will require a steadfastness in the face of delays or distractions.

School leaders can proactively support the implementation of SDI in myriad ways. Successful leaders present a clear vision of the "what" and the "why," integrating these so that everyone is motivated for the work. One without the other will leave participants feeling confused and impatient. Successful leaders also commit to gathering the necessary resources so that their team members have the right tools and don't become frustrated. Additionally, leaders honor and develop the talents of the team, both as individuals and as a group, looking for ways to sustain their energy for SDI over time. Leadership guarantees the power behind the promise!

11

Implement and Assess

Ironman events are filled with enthusiasm and energy as triathletes gather to endure a grueling 2.4-mile swim, a 112-mile bike ride, and, finally, a 26.2-mile marathon. Spectators and support teams line the courses, waving signs, cheering on their athletes, all with their fingers crossed for a good pace and finish time. The excitement is so contagious that observers often get caught up in the fever and announce their plans to sign up for the next one. This happened to me one brutally hot day in Chattanooga, TN as I watched several friends jump into the river to begin their long day. Luckily, I was wise enough to jump into my first Ironman experience with only a half-distance and on a relay team, committing myself to just the swim portion of the event. A few days later, the enormity of my commitment hit home while I was swimming laps in my local community pool. It was time to get serious about implementing a training plan and supporting my teammates with theirs.

Triathlon coach Joanna Zeiger advises newcomers to not worry too much about race day. "In reality, it is the conglomeration of all the workouts over the course of a training period that will lead to success." This advice must be sound, as Joanna is an Olympian and World Champion triathlete. Applying this advice to SDI is also sound – if the planning period has been thorough and thoughtful, and the team cohesive, then the roll-out is likely to be successful. Implementation without planning is like jumping in the river and swimming upstream, in the wrong direction! (See Figure 11.1.)

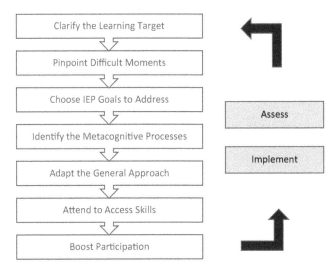

Figure 11.1 Implement and Assess

Implementation Roles

Special educators typically take the lead with implementation, providing most of the SDI. However, it is important to check the IEP to see who is listed as a service provider or support personnel. According to current federal law in the United States, any certified teacher can be responsible for SDI, including general educators, whereas special education teachers are responsible for reporting goal progress. State and local regulations may have different requirements, so it is important to know what commitment has been made to the family and student through the IEP process.

If a variety of team members – special and general education teachers, related professionals and paraeducators – will be working together to implement SDI, it is critical to share a clear instructional plan, provide training or direction as needed, and monitor student progress. Co-planning and co-delivery will ensure that everyone is instructing consistently and with fidelity to the plan. For students with disabilities, it is what we do consistently that will shape their success. Co-delivery has a naturally built-in monitoring system so that consistency can translate into goal attainment.

Co-delivery is especially important when paraeducators take on a significant role in SDI implementation. When I speak to paraeducators around the country, I often hear that they lack any face-to-face time with their special education teacher, communicating solely through student logs and data sheets. When I speak to special educators, I often hear that they have students on their caseload for whom they do progress monitoring, never having observed them in class, relying solely on information from a paraeducator.

Most paraeducators and special educators recognize that these practices are questionable at best, and alarming at worst. Persuasive advocacy is needed to develop schedules and caseloads that allow for the best collaboration practices to be carried out. Building a strong program now is easier than repairing damaged children later.

> Co-delivery has a naturally built-in monitoring system so that consistency can translate into goal attainment.

IEP Commitments

An Individual Education Program (IEP) will include key information about the frequency of services for a specific student. Regulations require that a child's team determine how many service minutes will be necessary to reach a specific set of goals. As team members consider this question, it is wise to remember the word *individual*. SDI minutes that are determined based on the daily bell schedule are not individualized. SDI minutes that are determined based on teacher availability are not individualized. Nor are minutes that are the exact same as the IEPs completed for all the other children in the building or with a similar diagnosis (e.g. Autism, Down Syndrome). Instead, educators should be recommending minutes based on careful reflection and professional judgment.

Each step in the IEP development process (strengths and needs, family concerns, etc.) provides key information that leads the team to an equitable decision regarding service time. Teams should avoid the temptation to skip any of these steps and come to a meeting with pre-determined minutes. After discussing each important IEP section and agreeing on goals, the team can then consider minutes of service.

The following process is an example of how one team determines SDI minutes.

1   Consider a goal and estimate the number of SDI minutes that will be required to bring that specific student to success by the end of the year.
2   Continue this process for each goal, and then total the estimated minutes.
3   Divide the total minutes by # of weeks or months in a school year. (Weekly or monthly minutes provide much greater flexibility than daily minutes.)
4   Recommend the weekly or monthly minutes to the IEP team.

As always, check with your local legal counsel or state regulations before adopting new IEP development practices.

IEP teams will also be indicating whether or not the service takes place with non-disabled peers. Federal law requires students to be served in the least restrictive environment. As teams discuss placement, the default should be to include students in general education settings, moving to separate settings only if absolutely necessary. Fortunately, SDI can be provided in any setting, as it is a service rather than a location. If the student will be receiving SDI within a general education setting, it will be helpful to complete a Planning Matrix, as described in Chapter 6 and illustrated in Table 6.2. With a Planning Matrix in place and available to all service providers working with a student, it will be easy to see where specific goals will be addressed and whether accommodations, modifications or SDI will be required.

With a well-written IEP in place, the team carries out the instructional plan they have developed for the week. While unexpected events may occur, the team strives for consistency and flexibility, communicating frequently with each other. The use of a shared, online document or logbook allows for quick updates throughout the week. Some teams reserve a few minutes at the start or end of each day to share quick summaries of student progress. Frequent communication will lead to winning practices for the team, and more importantly, for the student.

Implementation in Action

Anne Thurmond is a special education teacher at Powell Middle School in Littleton, Colorado. She feels fortunate to have been co-teaching math with Christina Dupen for several years. This consistent partnering has given them the time to develop confidence and trust. Thurmond's journey includes prior co-teaching experiences in which her expertise was not valued by the general education teacher. After reflecting on her own part in this, she realized that she needed to show more confidence during instruction and be ready to express her assessment of how the lesson was progressing. She encourages specialists to be professionally assertive during a lesson so that plans can be adjusted to provide a laser focus on student need.

Both teachers agree that flexibility is the key. Thurmond admits, "We come in with a plan but twenty minutes into the lesson we might have to say, 'This isn't working for a few students. Let's do some shifting.'" They recognize that it is important to continuously engage in formative assessment and analysis.

Dupen shares, "Sometimes it's a super small step forward while other times it is a bigger jump. You have to be flexible about meeting the student where they are at."

Their data support their approach, with almost all students making more than a year's growth in a year's time, and the majority of students with IEPs being ready for grade-level math classes when they enter high school. Not only do their students' academic scores improve, so does their confidence. Thurmond and Dupen survey their students at the beginning, middle and end of the year to gather a variety of information. While many students start the year writing comments such as "I hate math," by the end of the year their attitudes have changed. These students' comments capture the transformation that occurs.

> "I'm just really really glad I got this class, it's really helped me feel more comfortable with math. I use to be horrified to work on math before sixth grade and I was so embarrassed that I wasn't always great at it but now math doesn't bother me at all except for the fact that it can take a long time." Dalahi

> "I feel like I learn way much more when I am in small groups because then I feel like its easier for me to ask questions more and understand. Mrs. Dupen and Mrs. Thurmond always made sure we understood something and explained a concept more than once so we could get a hang of it and understand more." Brody

> "When I first switched to the class, I did not like to ask questions, but as the year went on, I asked questions every day." Noah

SDI is about more than just test scores. It is about providing students with the knowledge, skills and behaviors they need in order to experience a yearning for life-long learning. Thurmond and Dupen, along with dedicated teachers in classrooms around the world, show up every day to provide the "special" that makes this happen.

Assess For SDI

Progress on IEP goals is officially reported at the same time as student report cards are distributed. However, it is unwise to wait until that time to assess student progress. Instead, progress monitoring should be seen as an ongoing process designed to collect data that will inform instructional decisions, thereby improving the likelihood of success. Just as athletes look at their workout stats after every session to adjust their training plan, specialists should be frequently analyzing student data.

Baseline Data

Before an IEP is written, the specialist takes stock of a student's present levels of functioning. Once added to the IEP, this information is used to establish a baseline against which to judge progress. The method used to establish these levels should be the same method used to monitor student progress throughout the year. For example, if Dolch wordlists are used to assess a student's sight word vocabulary, then Dolch wordlists should be used for progress monitoring. This does not mean that additional data cannot be collected to inform instructional decisions. Quite the opposite is true. Multiple data sources provide a more robust picture of a student and decrease the chances of restrictive assessment tools interfering with accurate accounting.

Data Collection Methods

Assessments will vary enormously, based on the IEP goals for the student and any accommodations they may need. Most commonly, educators will use formative and summative assessment procedures. They may observe students responding in class, using gestures such as thumbs up, or holding up yes/no cards. They may use running records, oral interviews or computer probes. They may look at quizzes, tests and work products to glean progress or perform error analysis. In addition, specialists may need to gather data on IEP goals that aren't captured as easily in a paper product or computer-based test, such as social skills or behavior. In these cases, teachers may use direct methods of measurement, of which the four most common are duration, frequency, interval and anecdotal. Table 11.1 summarizes the uses of each.

Data Collection Roles

Anyone on the team can be involved in collecting data, but the primary responsibility for monitoring, analysis and adjustment lies with the special education teacher. The old adage, "Many hands make light work," is applicable for data collection, but, more importantly, a team approach will add authenticity to the information, creating a more robust picture. Data can show

Table 11.1 Direct Data Collection Methods

Type	Description	Possible Uses	How to Record
Duration	An exact measure of the length of time that something occurs	Any behavior that lasts awhile, such as: • Crying • On task/off task • Out of seat	Record specifically when the behavior begins and ends, using a clock or stopwatch.
Frequency	A tallying of the number of times something occurs	Any behavior that is a discreet, separate event, such as • Hitting • Work completion • Known vocabulary	List the time period for which you are counting behaviors. Tally the number of target behaviors.
Interval	A measure of something that takes place at either intentionally random or set intervals of time. Intervals are usually brief so that several take place during the time of observation.	Any behavior that you cannot observe constantly, such as • On task/off task • Daydreaming • Talking to neighbor	Choose the length of time interval (e.g. 5 minutes.) Look at the student every 5 minutes and record a + or – or a specific description of the behavior.
Anecdotal	Notes taken that describe specifically what the student did, often presented in an antecedent, behavior, consequence format.	Any behavior for which you are unsure of causes, or that is not measurable by other means, such as • Crawling under desks • Defiance or refusal • Voice volume while reading aloud	Keep track of time observed in your notes. Continually describe what is happening so that you will see what happened immediately before the behavior of concern and immediately afterward. If you were not observing before the behavior occurred, try to remember but mark it as "recalled."

how students respond in different settings with different service providers. This evidence can be extremely useful for teaching a student to generalize their skills to new or unexpected situations.

When paraeducators are involved, the specialist(s) must provide any necessary training and supervision of the data collection. Training might begin with showing the paraeducator various data collection examples, such as those shown in Tables 11.2–11.5. Next the paraeducator can shadow the specialist as they instruct and collect data. This can be followed by application practice with inter-rater reliability checks. Finally, the specialist should carefully review data taken by the paraeducator and occasionally observe to guarantee consistency.

Data Analysis

Consider the following questions when analyzing data contributed from *multiple team members*:

- Does the student respond differently in different settings?
- Does the student respond differently with different providers?
- Does the student respond differently around different peers?
- Does the student respond differently on different days or at different times of day?
- Does the student respond differently based on the task or curriculum context?
- What patterns do we detect?
- What were the antecedents and consequences? Were these impactful?
- Was the plan implemented with fidelity?

As we examine our data and ask these and other questions, we look for patterns that might inform our instructional decisions. Dylan William, world authority on assessment, asserts that when teachers do formative assessment *effectively*, students learn at almost double the rate. According to William, effective formative assessment is not so much about the methodology, but what is done with the evidence. Does the teacher adapt instruction based on individual student needs? Does the teacher provide feedback to the student while helping them to understand why they are receiving it and instructing them on how they can use it? If so, it will move the student more quickly toward the finish line. Data collection feeds back into our seven planning steps as we begin to think about our next lesson.

Table 11.2 Duration Data Example

Name: Rachel						
IEP Goal: Given silent work at her level, Rachel will increase vocal silence (decrease humming) to 8 minutes out of a 10-minute work period.						
Behavior: vocal silence, no humming						
Date	Observer	Setting	Start Time	End Time	Total Time	Comments
11/2	AM	Rm. 24	8:15	8:16:30	1 m 30s	Task-initiated
			8:16:30	8:19		humming
			8:20	8:22	2 m	Teacher nearby
			8:23	8:25		humming
					3 m 30s	Out of 10 min observation

Table 11.3 Frequency Data Example

Name: Keisha						
IEP Goal: Keisha will follow directions to remain seated during whole group instruction, decreasing out of seat incidents from an average of once per minute to once per 20 minutes.						
Behavior: Out-of-seat (without being directed by teacher)						
Date	Observer	Setting	Time Observed	Frequency/ Tallies	Total	Comments
10/15	KL	Rm. 120A	9:00-9:20	IIII	4	No smiles today
10/17	KL	Rm. 107	9:25-9:45	III	3	Sitting next to Bri
10/19	SW	Rm. 120A	9:00-9:20	IIIII II	7	Friday

Table 11.4 Interval Data Example

Name: Bryce														
IEP Goal: Bryce will increase on-task behavior (following teacher's direction for any activity within his readiness level) from current levels of 45% of the 50-minute period to 70%.														
Behavior: Working, pencil to paper, reading, looking at teacher, speaking with peers on topic														
Date	Observer	Setting	Time Observed	Interval length	1	2	3	4	5	6	7	8	9	10	Comments
3/7	JB	classroom	9:00–9:50	5 min	+	+	-	-	+	-	+	+	+	-	
3/8	JB	art room	1:00–1:50	5 min	+	+	-	-	-	-	+	-	-	+	Yawning, distracted by noise

Table 11.5 Anecdotal Data Example

Name: Tran
IEP Goal: Tran will remain in his seat unless otherwise directed, with only one out-of-seat incident per 45-minute class period.
Behavior: out-of-seat without permission
Observer – V.W.
Time Observed: 8:55 – 9:40
Setting: ELA Period 2

Date Time	Antecedent(s)	Behavior(s)	Consequence(s)
2/20 9:00	Mrs. B. with group at table up front; Tran at seat with raised hand but wasn't noticed by Mrs. B	Tran went up to Mrs. B.	Mrs. B. reminded him to stay in his seat and suggested he ask a friend for help
9:17	Mrs. B. at desk, conferencing with individual student	Tran went up to Mrs. B.'s desk.	Mrs. B. answered his question and he went back to his seat.
9:33	Mrs. B. leading mini-lecture using IWB. Tran fidgeting with pencil.	Tran got up to sharpen his pencil.	Mrs. B. continued with lecture.
9:34	Mrs. B. continuing with lecture.	Tran wandered back to seat from pencil sharpener, chatting to two students on his journey.	Mrs. B. said "Tran, stop talking and get back to your seat."

Time-Saving Tips

Many digital systems have been developed in the recent past to assist teachers with the task of collecting data. A quick internet search will yield dozens of apps and platforms, free and subscription-based, that can be customized for individual students. An initial investment of time setting up the systems can save significant time throughout the year. Some offerings have hardy security settings to protect student confidentiality while others do not. Check with your IT department to ensure that apps you are considering will meet the proper security standards.

There are also simple, no-tech data collection strategies that creative teachers have developed and shared for decades. A few favorites include:

◆ Adhere a two-inch piece of masking tape or an address label to your sleeve or wrist at the beginning of a lesson. This will make it simple to collect data as you circulate in the room, even if you don't have paper with you. Simply make tally marks on the tape and at the end of the lesson stick the tape or label onto the student's data chart.

◆ Purchase a hand-held tally counter. These are usually fitted with a ring to hold easily on your finger or hook at your waist. Tally behaviors throughout the period with a simple tap of the finger.

◆ Create data collection charts small enough to fit on index cards. Punch a single hole in the corner of each card and hang these on a key ring. Whoever is working with the student(s) can hook the ring onto a belt loop, lanyard or over a wheelchair handle and have the necessary forms with them at all times.

◆ Set up a data collection schedule for the team. For example, on Monday and Thursdays, data are collected on Goals 3 and 5, while on Tuesdays and Fridays, data are collected on Goals 1, 2 and 4. This provides a focus so that no one feels overwhelmed by the task.

◆ Add a data collection symbol to the Planning Matrix (described in Chapter 6). Distribute the data collection tasks throughout the week in meaningful locations and times. Or simply print a new copy of the matrix each week and highlight the times when data collection will be expected.

◆ Engage students in gathering data for you and for themselves. Show them how to tally behaviors, create a graph or in some other way self-monitor (see self-monitoring example in Chapter 9.) Not only does this save some time; it is also an excellent way to teach students to become more independent in their learning.

1	2	3	4	5	6	7	8	9	10

1	2	3	4	5	6	7	8	9	10
1	2	3	4	5	6	7	8	9	10
1	2	3	4	5	6	7	8	9	10
1	2	3	4	5	6	7	8	9	10
1	2	3	4	5	6	7	8	9	10

Figure 11.2 Data Strips

- ◆ If you have a set of 10 questions you are asking several students, provide them each with a strip of ten boxes. Then, ask them to color in the questions they answered correctly. Simply line up the strips to see your patterns! (Figure 11.2)

Whichever approach you use to collect data, remember that the process is about more than just collecting! As marketing and data guru Jim Bergeson says, "Data will talk to you if you're willing to listen." Listen up to power up your specially designed instruction!

To Sum Up

- ◆ Specially designed instruction can occur in many different settings and be implemented by a variety of team members. While the special education teacher takes on the primary role, co-delivery is most effective for students.
- ◆ SDI minutes can be written in ways that allow flexible instruction throughout a week or month. This flexibility can be especially helpful in inclusive settings.
- ◆ Assessment's main purpose should be to inform instruction so that the student progresses as quickly as possible toward the goal. All team members can be involved in collecting data, but the special educator is primarily responsible for progress monitoring reports.

Reflection Questions

- ◆ How do you determine service minutes for the IEP? How might you improve that process?
- ◆ What tools is your team using to collect data on IEP goals? Are there related student behaviors or access skills that you should collect data on to give you a more robust picture of the student?
- ◆ Do you enjoy data analysis? If not, why not? What can make the analysis step more appealing?

Try This

◆ Select a student (or family member) and collect data using one of the methods that you are least confident in, e.g. interval recording or an ABC anecdotal record. Jot a quick reflection afterward about the experience.

◆ Do an internet search for data collection tips for teachers. Hundreds of recommendations will pop up! Choose two ideas to test out, and then share your experience with others.

12

Leadership for SDI

Many of us can envision the pleasure of roasting marshmallows over an outdoor campfire. What do you see? Perhaps a few family members sit in a circle around the firepit, swapping ghost stories, singing songs or catching fireflies. Or perhaps a large group of friends engage in hilarious conversation that lasts deep into the night. These picturesque Americana moments are immediately appealing to me, but I catch myself and remember the work required to turn the idea into reality. First, we need to establish a clear enough vision of our desired outcome for the evening. Then, just to have a successful fire, the best tinder must be gathered and ignited. The initial, hesitant flames need to be fanned gently in order to grow. Once the fire is established, it must be stoked continuously with more wood and shored up so that it doesn't dissipate. Achieving a memorable campfire experience requires translating our vision into concrete, actionable steps. For SDI to become a glowing, energy-producing component of your service continuum you must begin by establishing a vision and then develop a plan for gathering resources, fanning the first flames, stoking and fueling, and shoring up special education practices.

Establishing A Vision

Vision, as described by organizational psychologist Stuart Freedman, must be "rooted in your past, address the future, and deal with today's realities. It represents who you are and what you stand for. It inspires you, and the people whose commitment you need, to act to make constructive change towards a future you all want to see" (2008).

Education leaders must have a clear vision of the future they want to see for students with disabilities and articulate this to their community. With a Windex-like shine, this vision must not be blotted by smudges and hard-to-see-through streaks, but instead be crystal clear to all who will provide services to students. The following questions can help to polish your vision as it relates to specially designed instruction:

◆ Do I want to design something new or reinforce the familiar?
◆ Do I believe that "all" belong to our school community? What do I really mean by all?
◆ Do I see students with disabilities as an integral part of our success and community life?
◆ How do I view the interaction of general and special education?
◆ Do I focus on capacities before deficits? Is my understanding of capacity flexible enough and open to new ways of thinking about students' gifts?
◆ Do I have high expectations for students with disabilities? Academic? Behavioral? Social?
◆ Do I expect special education teachers to be providing something special that is also rigorous enough to challenge students with disabilities?
◆ Do I hold the same high expectations for quality instruction from special education teachers as I do for general education teachers?
◆ Do I believe that collaborative efforts will cause students with disabilities to be more successful than ever?

Gathering Resources

Most districts will have the obvious resources in place – special education staff, basic training modules and guides, IEP procedures, curriculum and classroom essentials. However, if insanity is doing the same thing over and over again and expecting different results, then leaders will want to explore what new or different resources might be needed for success. Two proactive processes – perspective mapping and resource curation - may point you in the right direction.

Perspective Mapping
Perspective mapping provides a structure for considering the perspectives of the parties that are involved with an issue. This is especially critical when it feels as if people are being asked to make a change to the old ways of

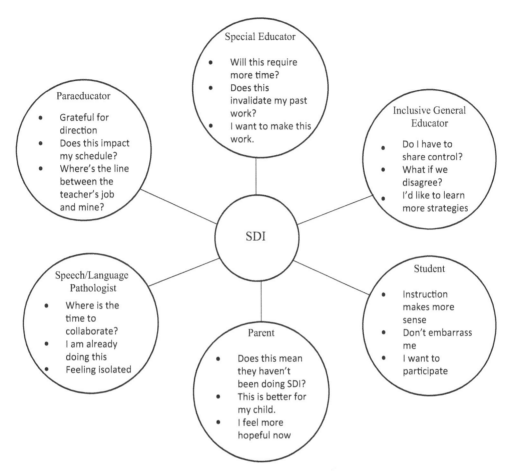

Figure 12.1 SDI Perspective Map Example

operating. As Alyssa Gallagher and Kami Thordarson point out in *Design Thinking for School Leaders*, change is scary, with people often needing time to grieve the things that they feel are lost in the process (2018). Some specialists may be anxious, scared or overwhelmed with a new emphasis on SDI. While our personal perspective might be one of excitement and growth, it is foolhardy to assume that everyone shares the same perspective. Gaining empathy through perspective mapping can be eye-opening.

To create a perspective map, you can use a "bubble thinking map," a web or a table. Place the issue or topic in the middle, and then create outlying areas for each perspective you want to consider. For the best outcome, interview each of the parties to find out their perspective on SDI, but also be ready to make educated guesses about various perspectives if needed. Try to see it through the eyes of the other. What will be their concerns? What will they embrace? As an alternative, consider inviting your stakeholders to help you create a perspective map together. Encourage their honest input so that your plans can be based on a solid foundation. Figure 12.1 illustrates an example of an SDI Perspective Map. Yours may end up being similar or looking very different. It is important to not simply adopt this one, but to create one that accurately reflects your own circumstances.

The first person to use the phrase "Walk a mile in their shoes" has been lost to history while the saying is alive and well. Its timeless message of empathy applies whether the shoes are heels, sneakers or hiking boots! As thought leader Jethro Jones writes, "When a stakeholder interacts with the school in a way that decreases the enjoyment or quality of their experience, you need to find out how they feel about that. Saying, 'I think they feel this way' isn't good enough. You must *feel* what it is like to be in their shoes" (2020, p. 10).

Many school leaders have worn the shoes of a general education teacher, but fewer have taken on the role of special educator. To improve your perspective map, consider putting on a special education teacher's shoes and planning a lesson according to the seven steps for SDI. How easy or difficult is it? How much time did it require? What resources did you need? Not only will your perspective shift, your credibility with your special education team will soar.

Co-Planning Time

A completed perspective map can now guide your decisions about the resources you need to gather. As found in Figure 12.1, time for collaborative planning is of high concern to most educators. Arranging for adequate co-planning time is one of the greatest gifts a school leader can offer. How do we find the time? Schools all over the country are grappling with this question. Some of the solutions they find are small, short-term fixes, while others are more systemic, addressing the problem on a long-term basis. Ideally, common planning time will be built into the regular school day, sometimes by the strategic use of specials or by asking schedulers to place a priority on common planning periods for co-teachers. When this is not possible, school leaders get creative.

One creative solution is often referred to as the "Roaming Sub Strategy." Once a month, a sign-up sheet is sent to co-teachers, divided into two columns, with 30- or 45-minute time blocks down the left-hand side. General education teachers write their name in one of the blocks in the left-hand column, and the name of their specialist in the opposite block. One or two substitutes are brought in to cover for the teachers, roaming in short time blocks from class to class throughout the day.

Smart leaders have also found another way to utilize substitutes—without additional expenses. When a substitute covers for a teacher, there is usually a period (or two) during the day designated as a prep. Because substitutes don't do "prep," their time is usually spent waiting for the minute hand to move along. Some principals have recognized this wasted resource and are putting substitutes to work during the prep period by having them support or cover for a co-teacher. Office staff can be enlisted to make these arrangements in the morning as soon as a teacher has called in sick.

Many schools have a day each week where they hold several meetings in a row to develop Individualized Education Plans (IEPs) for students in special education. Typically, a substitute is brought in so that general education teachers can attend the meetings. If these meetings do not fill the entire day, the substitute can cover a co-teacher's class so that she has an additional planning opportunity. In addition, when substitutes are brought in for a half-day of meetings, some schools decide to hire the person for the entire day. The difference in cost is usually minimal, yet it can yield several extra hours of coverage for collaboration activities.

Finding time for teachers and paraeducators to collaborate without students present can be complicated by work schedules. Districts often contract with paraeducators to work the same hours that students attend school. The cost-free solution? Allow paraeducators to flex their schedule by thirty minutes one day each week, arriving either a half-hour earlier or staying a half-hour later. Providing a choice of day and time will probably accommodate most paraeducators' home demands and allow the team to cover students for the thirty minutes of arrival or departure activities. In a few cases, you may need to consult IEP commitments regarding full-time paraeducator support to students.

Resource Curation

Resource curation is a process that brings together a group of stakeholders to identify current resources related to an issue and organize them for ease of use. Technology provides many tools for curating resources online so that they can be accessible to all parties. Begin by setting up a shared folder or site, determining a clear purpose for this repository, and creating desired categories and subcategories. For example, educators might recognize a need for more ideas on how to address executive function deficits. This category can be broken down into the subcategories found in Table 9.1. As team members come across a helpful idea or website on executive functions, they can add it to the appropriate subcategory. In addition, if a team member has a set of hands-on materials to share or demonstrate, he can list them in a subcategory along with his contact information.

The curation and sharing of ideas is essential for specialists who are the only one of their type in a building or district. A solo special education teacher in an elementary school is more likely to struggle with designing effective adaptations than one in a larger building with colleagues nearby. A speech/language pathologist who is the only one in a secondary school will need structures that connect her with other SLPs to brainstorm solutions. In addition, new or less experienced teachers will greatly appreciate a repository of resources, meaningfully organized.

Policies and Procedures

UDL experts Patti Kelly Ralabate and Elizabeth Berquist recommend a similar process, *resource mapping*, to explore organizational policies and procedures that might need updating. Thinking about resources in this way, leaders might start to ask questions about job descriptions, such as

- Is the job description sufficiently clear regarding the provision of SDI?
- Does the job description include a focus on collaboration?
- Do job descriptions make clear who is responsible for directing and supervising paraeducators?

Leaders may also examine teacher evaluation protocols and forms to assess whether they are sufficiently differentiated for the role of the special educator or related professional. It is not enough to observe that special education teachers are instructing in ways that have been identified as effective in a general education classroom. They *must* be doing something special. Evaluation protocols that clarify this will lead to better outcomes for students with disabilities.

> It is not enough to observe that special education teachers are instructing in ways that have been identified as effective in a general education classroom. They *must* be doing something special.

Fanning the First Flames

You've gathered your SDI resources – a small stack of kindling artfully arranged, with larger pieces of dry wood off to the side. You've realized the potential of more effective SDI and you are eager to spread your initial flame of enthusiasm. You realize that piling large, dense pieces on top will douse the fire, so instead it's time to gently fan the motivation in others.

Motivation for SDI

Susan Fowler, a researcher and professor in leadership, poses a Spectrum of Motivation model for change events (2014). The six motivational outlooks include:

- Disinterested
- External
- Imposed
- Aligned
- Integrated
- Inherent

The first three of these outlooks are considered sub-optimal, whereas motivational outlooks that are aligned, integrated or inherent are referred to as "motivational health food" or optimal.

> Aligned – the ability to link the task to something you value, such as learning
> Integrated – the ability to link the task to a current, relevant purpose
> Inherent – a natural interest in or enjoyment of the type of task presented

Fowler's research has found that when the psychological needs of "autonomy, relatedness and competence are satisfied, the result is an aligned, integrated or inherent motivational outlook" (44). Special educators usually have a fair amount of autonomy in their work, at least outside of the realm of federal and state mandates. In fact, many special education teachers wish for more direction! To fan motivation for the work of SDI, make relatedness and competence a part of your action plan.

Relatedness

Humans need connectedness – to others and to the work. As mentioned previously, many specialists are isolated in their roles. Leaders can actively support staff by structuring relationship opportunities. In a simple fashion, these relationships can be through one-to-one networking. Principals and district leaders often have a better awareness than teachers of staff who work at buildings other than their own. Consider who might make a good partner or mentor and connect the pair by email or in-person introductions. In the introduction, be sure to include the specific reason for the match, i.e. experience with students with complex bodies or an interest in early literacy. Then step back and let the relationship develop on its own.

In a more organized fashion, a district-wide Professional Learning Community (PLC) dedicated to SDI will provide a sustaining structure of multiple connections. An SDI PLC might be initiated by a district-level special education leader, a school building principal or a teacher-leader trying to meet her own needs. Independent of who initiates the PLC, district support will be necessary to sustain it over time. This may include a meeting space, after school energy snacks, continuing education credits or stipends for hours beyond the workday.

Allow PLC members to develop their own norms and protocols, and be clear that the purpose is collaboration, not competition; support not judgment. Many of the members will feel vulnerable as they admit to a less-than-robust understanding of SDI or ask for ideas. The group may need to meet frequently, at first, to develop a sense of community and trust, as well as to prove the group value to each individual. As the PLC takes hold, meeting schedules may be adjusted to reflect the group's needs.

Several social media groups exist for special educators around the world to connect. While these provide opportunities to receive hundreds of responses to a question or request for help, a word of caution is necessary. Posts in these groups often reveal misunderstandings of SDI, accommodations, modifications and other responsibilities of a legal nature. With the best of intentions, advice is often given that appears contrary to what the law requires. Encourage teachers to use these sites with professional prudence.

Competence

We all have a need to learn and grow. As young children, we eagerly persevered through the steps required to learn complex tasks – walking, pulling on a shirt, tying shoelaces – often while shouting loud, adamant demands of "I do it!" Accomplishment has an almost addictive quality to it, as our brains flood with dopamine when we notice ourselves making progress toward a goal. In contrast, feeling incompetent can bring a sense of shame. Psychologist Jena Field explains that shame brings about a fear response, as our brain releases stress hormones designed to protect us (2017). These protective measures can include blaming, denying, justifying and avoidance – often referred to as the "fight or flight" response. These are the kinds of behaviors that will put out a fire in record time.

Pre-service programs do their best to provide schools with specialists who are competent and confident. However, all pre-service programs have to choose among dozens of competing priorities to fit into the limited number of hours of coursework. Every college in the country will have exposed special educators to the concept of SDI, but informal surveying shows that it is usually a cursory overview provided during an overwhelming course on laws and the IEP. Methods courses may give SDI another quick glance, but until teacher candidates have real-life application opportunities it can be hard to make sense of.

Experienced special educators may also have an underdeveloped sense of SDI. Those that have worked in a self-contained setting may have been following a scripted, alternate curriculum, with no need to actively design their own specialized instruction. Those working in inclusive settings may have been given the impression that they were to "help" students, rather than "teach," or that they were to look like a general education teacher. They may be under the false assumption that accommodations such as notetaking guides, individualized schedules or extra praise qualify as SDI. To exacerbate this, years of positive evaluations may have reinforced their sense that what they were doing was enough.

As I work with districts around the country on SDI, I encounter many specialists who are surprised and concerned by the expectations I share. I delicately try to balance the kindling as I fan the flames. Through carefully planned professional learning activities, we can maintain and build upon the competence that already exists, while motivating educators to improve their practices.

Professional Learning

Professional learning is most effective when it is customized to individual needs and entered into by choice. However, the truth is that there are times when mandatory training is justified. Just as we mandate school safety training because of its life and death consequences, so too we can consider basic SDI training to have significant consequences. In this case, providing choice about the vehicle for the information can still address adults' need for control over their learning.

In addition to traditional workshop events, consider offering one or more of the following alternatives (or supplements) to guarantee that all staff have the necessary knowledge and skills.

- ◆ Flipped Lessons – Just like with students, a flipped lesson allows learners to participate at their own time and place. Find or create a slideshow or video about SDI. Use a video tool such as EdPuzzle to embed reflection or retrieval questions in the middle and at the end.
- ◆ Visits – Observing other specialists (in the building, district or neighboring district) is a valuable way to reflect on what works and what doesn't. Guided visits, with focused observation questions, usually work best for those that are new to the field.

◆ Book Study – Self-paced reading, or with a group, can provide much fodder for reflection and discussion. Ask participants to each take on responsibility for facilitating discussion about a chapter. Joint ownership will increase the commitment to the study process.

◆ WebQuest – Create a list of SDI-related websites for teachers to explore. A quick internet search yields hundreds of options. Infuse some fun by setting up teams to do a competitive scavenger hunt with a web tool such as GooseChase at www.goosechase.com.

◆ Virtual Interviews – Talk with an expert for a few minutes using a virtual conferencing tool such as Skype, Zoom or FaceTime. Micro-learning, a short burst of learning time, is an attractive option for busy professionals. Plus, experts are often willing to give a few minutes of their time for free to support inclusive practices.

Stoking and Fueling

Every fire needs continual fueling or it will die out. Sustainability of SDI practices is not optional. Legal and ethical imperatives make it clear that cursory efforts are not enough. Leaders will want to plan for ongoing support through coaching and resource expansion.

Coaching

Receiving real-time feedback on SDI practices helps specialist translate workshop information into daily instruction. External coaches bring an outside perspective, often able to identify areas for growth based on regional or national practices. Many districts use an external coach for two or three visits during the first and second years of SDI revitalization. Internal coaches can provide more frequent feedback and support, while also connecting specialists with others in the school or district that have similar needs or creative solutions.

Coaching will be most well-received from someone with credibility in SDI. However, the coaching process does not require an expert, and can be effectively applied by using some of the following discussion questions.

General coaching questions for SDI:

◆ Do you have a shared online lesson planning form with your team?
◆ Is your lesson planning form working as well as you'd like? If not, why?
◆ What does a typical planning session look like for you?
◆ Which of the seven SDI planning steps is most challenging for you?

- What method are you using to keep the IEP or other student goals in front of you for lesson planning?
- How do you usually address these goals during the lesson?
- How frequently are you addressing IEP goals?
- What are some of the executive functions that your students need in order to access the standards?
- Which students need accommodations or modifications? How do you keep these in mind?
- Which small instructional group configurations are you using? Why?
- What strategies are you using to boost student participation?
- How are you communicating IEP goals and accommodations to paraeducators?
- What is an example of specially designed instruction (SDI) that you have implemented in the past week?
- What does your progress monitoring show? How do you bring this into team discussions and lesson planning?

Coaching questions for after a lesson observation:

- Did you provide SDI today? If so, what did it entail?
- How did you address the IEP goals during the lesson?
- What type of changes did you make to the lesson to boost participation by students with disabilities?
- What was your sense of student engagement?
- Did you make any changes on the fly? What and why?
- Why did you choose the specific small-group configurations you used today? Would you do it differently?
- How did you assess progress today on IEP goals?
- What formative assessment methods did you use today? How well did they work?
- Based on what you experienced today, what type of SDI might your students with disabilities need for the next lesson?
- Can you think of ways to adapt print material, lectures or discussions that would make them more accessible to students with IEPs?
- What might "better" look like to you?

While coaching is typically linked to a lesson observation, it can also generate substantial results when applied to the planning process. Coaches can offer to sit with a specialist and plan a lesson together using the seven steps described in earlier chapters. Doing so affords the opportunity to notice steps that are strengths and steps that are weaknesses, so that ongoing support can be directed with precision. If the specialist is co-planning, coaches can offer to observe the partners' process, then guide them to reflect using some of the previous questions.

Resource Expansion

Special education teachers sometimes feel that their bag of tricks has a whole in the bottom of it. Just when they have filled it up, believing they have the knowledge and skills for success, a new student arrives carrying never-before-seen needs. Teachers scramble to pull a strategy or solution from their bag, only to dig down unsuccessfully. Sustainability of SDI practices requires that specialists have a growth mindset for themselves, stay on top of the latest research, and continuously seek new ideas. Leaders can support resource expansion by implementing one of the following steps.

> Sustainability of SDI practices requires that specialists have a growth mindset for themselves, stay on top of the latest research, and continuously seek new ideas.

◆ If your professional library subscribes to education journals, check to see if there are any subscriptions for special education journals. A similar check can be done for professional books. Be sure that dollars are being spent equitably so all staff have the latest news from their profession. Don't have a budget line for a school-based library of journals? Send an email request to the district-level special education administrator requesting a donation of recent publications that they have finished reading.

◆ Approach the SDI PLC you have fostered and invite them to take turns with an Idea of the Month newsletter. This can be as simple as linking to a blog or vlog, an article or a Pinterest board. Assist them in creating a district-wide email list of staff that would benefit.

◆ Show your appreciation of teachers by publicizing strong SDI practices you find during classroom visits. Notice a specialist doing something innovative in math? Take a photo, write a short blurb and share it with others. Ever-present mobile devices make this easy to do on-the-spot, before other pressing demands make us forget. Testimonials of this type, especially when paired with student success data, will really stoke the fire!

◆ Develop a list of resources that highlight evidence-based practices so that specialists can uphold the legal requirement to be evidence-based whenever possible. The Council for Exceptional Children, a leading professional organization, shares videos, articles and podcasts on their website, www.exceptionalchildren.org. Corwin, publisher of John Hattie's research, hosts a website packed with proven practices at www.visiblelearningmetax.com. The What Works Clearinghouse reviews existing research on educational programs and practices and posts approved examples at www.ies.ed.gov/ncee/wwc. The American Speech-Language-Hearing Association provides evidence maps for all things related to SLP services at https://www.asha.org/Evidence-Maps/. Other sites exist, so make your document accessible and editable so that SDI team members can contribute as they find new sources.

◆ Encourage specialists to make SDI a component of their professional growth plan for their evaluation cycle. Professional growth plans are a personal commitment to action, with a comprehensive set of steps to advance teaching and learning. Given that specially designed instruction is the foremost role of a special education teacher, it follows that their professional growth plan would make this a priority.

Shoring Up

A master fire builder maintains a watchful eye, observing for weak areas and pre-emptively shoring them up. Maintaining a campfire long enough to outlast the marshmallows and tall tales requires an evaluative diligence and readiness to respond. Services for students with disabilities also deserve attentive diligence and responsiveness from school leaders. Sonya Kunkel, special education administrator and national expert on inclusive practice, says, "SDI is our art and data is our science." We must examine not only our art, but also our data, looking at it from a variety of angles to ensure that our efforts are working and sustainable. (See Chapter 11 for more information about data collection on individual students.)

Evaluations

Program evaluations can take many forms, focusing on students, teachers, classrooms, school-based programs or district-wide services. Generally, these evaluations look for trends and patterns related to effectiveness. They also can be used to identify inequities or compliance issues. Analysts may examine things such as referrals, test scores, IEPs, placements and suspensions. Comprehensive in nature, they typically look beyond the issue of SDI, to incorporate other facets of special education services, and are beyond the scope of this book.

The SDI Success Checklist (Table 12.1) contains thirty facets of SDI as they relate to service provider preparation and practice. Each facet has been more

Table 12.1 SDI Success Checklist

1=Strongly Disagree, 2=Partly Disagree, 3=Neutral or Unknown, 4=Partly Agree, 5=Strongly Agree

Special education teachers and related professionals...	1	2	3	4	5
1 have a clear understanding of SDI.					
2 have adequate resources to provide SDI.					
3 have adequate time to plan for SDI.					
4 have a capacity-driven mindset about students with disabilities.					
5 have an "our students" vs. "my students" mindset.					
6 have a structure for collaborating with other specialists.					
7 develop relationships with parents/ guardians to support SDI practices.					
8 understand role in directing and supervising paraeducators in implementing SDI.					
9 direct and supervise paraeducators as needed for implementation of SDI.					
10 understand role of collaborator with any general educators that teach students with IEPs.					
11 communicate accommodations, modifications and SDI practices to general education colleagues in a clear and timely manner.					
12 engage in courageous conversations with colleagues in order to meet the needs of students with disabilities.					
13 develop relationships with students that foster efficient learning.					
14 embed universal design for learning practices when planning for group instruction to reduce the need for SDI.					
15 adapt content as necessary, while still maintaining high expectations.					
16 adapt methodology and delivery in ways that are clearly special.					

(Continued)

Special education teachers and related professionals...	1	2	3	4	5
17 can articulate which IEP goals are being addressed in a given lesson.					
18 use evidence-based instructional practices to the extent possible.					
19 incorporate multiple learning modalities to increase effectiveness of instruction for students with disabilities.					
20 use methods designed to boost student participation in lessons.					
21 instruct students on necessary executive function strategies to increase access and success.					
22 collect and analyze formative and summative data.					
23 provide students with specific and timely feedback.					
24 share relevant data with team members.					
25 ascertain sufficient progress on IEP goals.					
26 respond to a lack of progress by making informed changes.					
27 stay abreast of research in special-education-related topics.					
28 have a wealth of instructional strategies to use with students.					
29 actively seek out new resources to use for SDI.					
30 willingly accept feedback on SDI practices and take steps to improve.					

thoroughly explained throughout the previous chapters. School leaders who have familiarized themselves with those detailed explanations might use this checklist as the basis for a professional learning discussion outlining the SDI expectations for specialists. Clarity of expectations has been shown by neuroscientists to cause our brains to enter into a highly productive state (Zak 2017). Other research shows that employee attitudes are more positive when their employers have clarified expectations for them (Amabile and Kramer 2011). Taking the time to clarify SDI expectations will yield team members who are more constructive in their work.

The checklist may also be used to informally evaluate how prepared and skilled school special education teachers and related professionals are, as a group or as individuals. Alternatively, an individual specialist may choose to use the checklist, substituting the word "I" in front of each statement. Where scores are strong, leaders can congratulate, celebrate and consider how to utilize these strengths for the good of all. Where specific scores are low, leaders can shore up with many of the strategies previously mentioned. Where scores are concerning, leaders can follow normal administrative protocols such as improvement plans.

The specialists I meet in my day-to-day work are inquisitive, dedicated, solution-seekers. They truly want to do what is best for children. With the right kind of leadership, they will give our students with disabilities something truly special.

To Sum Up

◆ Effective leaders reflect on their vision for students with disabilities and then share it publicly. In doing so, they ignite a spark for constant improvement in special education services.

◆ Leaders organize a variety of structures to enhance services. These may include perspective mapping, resource curation, co-planning schedules, and a review of policies and procedures. To motivate others, leaders foster connections and competence through professional learning opportunities and coaching. Finally, they integrate evaluation strategies to help everyone see where they are and where they need to be going.

Reflection Questions

◆ How well do you, as a leader, understand SDI? If not currently a leader, how well do you think your administration understands the concept? How might you improve this?

◆ What resources do you use to stay current on research about learners with disabilities? How might you fit time into your schedule to review research briefs or dive deeply into a specific topic that would advance learning for these students?

◆ Who do you network with to share ideas related to special education and SDI? Are there other people that you can reach out to? Do any existing networks already exist that you can join?

Try This

- ◆ Create a perspective map for the SDI stakeholders in your school. What do you believe they will think and feel about a revitalized emphasis on specially designed instruction? Engage in some conversations to see if your predictions were accurate.
- ◆ Explore websites that address specially designed instruction. Make a list of five to ten that might be helpful to educators as they try to improve their SDI practices. And, if you're feeling creative, turn it into a WebQuest!

13

Conclusion

I grew up in a quiet, low-income suburb of Washington, D.C. Our home, like most of our neighbors, was very modest, without air conditioning or fancy furnishings, but filled with love. Washington, D.C. in the summer is as humid as a sauna, so as soon as the dinner meal was finished and dishes were washed and put away, most of the neighbors would venture outside to try to catch a bit of breeze. Children played tag and ball in the quiet street as the parents chatted with each other, still keeping a watchful eye on us.

Directly across the street from me lived a tall, good-looking eighteen-year-old boy named Wayne. Not only was he athletically agile, but he was kind to all of us younger kids, carrying the little ones piggyback style and throwing a football back and forth with my brothers. Everyone loved Wayne. One day in the summer of his eighteenth year, a letter arrived at Wayne's home announcing he had been called up for service in Vietnam. While most of us were devastated by this news, Wayne seemed to grow in stature, accepting the call with pride as he went off to serve his country.

Summer turned to a cooling fall, followed by an icy winter. Eventually the crocus began to push through the ground about the time that the mailman delivered another letter to Wayne's home, this time announcing that he would be returning from Vietnam early. He had stepped on a land mine and lost his leg.

Several months passed while Wayne was in the hospital followed by a rehabilitation center, sending letters to his parents who generously shared his progress with all of us. Then, one night my parents shook me awake and told me to put on my bathrobe and shoes and follow them outside. Startled and a bit scared, I managed to quickly don something respectable and went to the front door. Although it was dark outside, the streetlamp cast a broad circle of light onto the road, and right in the middle of that circle sat Wayne in his wheelchair. He had just returned home for the very first time. News spread like wildfire through the neighborhood and in just minutes the street was filled with adults and children wanting to welcome him home. As the fathers went to shake his hand, Wayne insisted on standing up to do so. Even though they encouraged him to stay seated, he insisted on standing on just one leg as he restarted his life in our community.

Wayne was the first person I ever knew to have a disability, and I am so grateful to him. As he went on to become a high diver, as he played street football with my brothers, as he greeted the day with a smile, he showed me that capacity is so much deeper than what is seen on the surface. I learned that when we tap into capacities that may be initially hidden, amazing things happen. My sense of disability began with a "can-do" mindset rather than a "can't-do" one.

> When we tap into capacities that may be initially hidden, amazing things happen.

Specially designed instruction (SDI) unveils student capacities in a way that nothing else can, as long as the educators and students have a "can-do" mindset. As mentioned in Chapter 3, the concept of least dangerous assumption applies to SDI. We can either assume competence, with all of the many positive opportunities it brings, or we can assume incompetence and hold low expectations, foster dependence and limit opportunities.

Throughout the chapters we explored examples of SDI teams that expanded opportunities for students by thoughtfully designing instruction. They carefully considered the learning targets and inherent challenges in the curriculum. They were very intentional about which IEP goals to integrate and monitor. They were reflective about metacognition, adaptations, access skills and executive function. And to make the lesson even more powerful, they embedded strategies for boosting participation. By combining all of these considerations, they created lessons brimming with opportunities. They moved beyond "can do" to "we did it!"

I often wonder what it might be like to hold a conversation today with my neighbor, Wayne. If I asked him about his mindset, I believe he would tell me that he knew instinctually that the opposite of a capacity-focused mindset was too dark and dangerous a path for him, leading to a life of failure and unfulfilled dreams. So, too, we must imagine the dark and dangerous paths our students will travel if we do not instill in ourselves and in them a sense of capacity and desire for growth. I believe that educators do want this for the children they serve, but sometimes lose sight of how to provide it. The planning steps presented in this book can serve as lampposts along the path, illuminating the journey so that everyone arrives at their learning destination.

Appendix A

Additional SDI Examples

Wise educators experience a slight hesitation before grabbing a strategy that sounds simple and engaging. They know that the process of specially designed instruction requires them to consider the unique needs of the child with a disability and their IEP goals when planning learning experiences. As you peruse the examples* in this appendix, pause for a moment and consider what you know of the individual students you teach.

- What is the IEP goal you are addressing?
- Does the idea fit with what you know about the student's learning profile?
- Is the idea supported by research?
- Is there an idea that might be a better fit?
- Are there ways to tweak it to fit your student's needs?

The examples in this chapter are described as possible interventions for several different IEP goals. These goals are listed in an abbreviated fashion, without the success criteria that would be individualized based on a student. The list of example goals is not all inclusive, as each strategy may apply to many other goals and circumstances.

While the directions for each example are written as SDI for one student, there may be several students in the class (or all!) that would benefit from the intervention. It is usually most efficient to pull a few students with common IEP goals into a small group. If the collaborative team feels that other students (without IEPs) would benefit from the lesson, those students would be receiving incidental benefit rather than SDI.

Creativity and flexibility are strengths when developing specially designed instruction. Feel free to tweak these ideas to better suit your students' needs and your teaching style. Keep track of any adjustments you make for quick reference in the future.

*Other examples have been sprinkled throughout the book. They are not duplicated in this appendix.

Distinction Pockets

Thinking at Every Desk is a well-read book on my teacher bookshelf. Authors Derek Cabrera and Laura Colosi explain the four basic thinking skills that students need – Distinctions, Relationships, Systems and Patterns (DRSP). These skills are required for basic survival and for school success, as they cut across every content and grade level. Students with disabilities often struggle because they have difficulty grasping one or more of these skills, especially in a concrete way. Teachers who create ways to make these thinking categories more explicit will be sure to help students succeed. This strategy provides scaffolding and practice for students while making their thinking about distinctions very visible.

Selected IEP goal:

◆ *Choose text evidence to support a claim…*

Other possible IEP goals:

◆ Recognize key characteristics of familiar objects…
◆ Identify similarities and differences…
◆ Understand and follow classroom/school rules…
◆ Define and compare attributes of geometric shapes…

How to:

1 Obtain a heavy-duty page protector and cut off the top third. Dispose of this piece.
2 Draw a line down the center with a permanent marker. Mark "not" on the right side as seen in Figure A.1.
3 While choosing text evidence is the end goal, begin by building their understanding of making distinctions. Explain that the learning target for the lesson is "I can make distinctions among familiar things."
4 Print and cut out several small images, some of living things, some not.
5 With a dry erase marker, write "Living" on the left side.
6 Direct the student to make a distinction between living things and non-living, by placing the images in the pocket on one side or the other. When the student is finished, discuss with them how they made the distinctions and then remove the images.

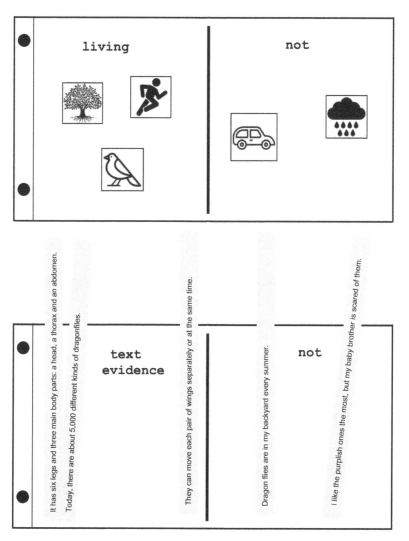

Figure A.1 Distinction Pockets

7 Provide the student with a collection of words printed on small cards, including a variety of parts of speech. Explain that we make distinctions among words as well.

8 Erase the left side of the pocket and write "nouns." Ask the student to distinguish between nouns and "not" nouns by placing the words in the pocket. Provide positive and corrective feedback as needed.

9 If the student is successful as understanding distinctions, move on to making distinctions between evidence that supports a claim and "not." Label the left side of the pocket "Supporting Evidence."

10 Present the student with a claim about the text on a piece of paper or whiteboard. Explain that they will take what they know about making distinctions and apply it to text evidence.

11 Provide the student with sentence strips taken from the text, some that are supportive and others that are not. Model the process with one sentence strip, thinking aloud as you place it in the distinction pocket. Ask the student to do the next one with you and move toward independent practice when ready.

Other considerations:

◆ Because this strategy builds a sense of efficacy, be sure to choose items that the student will be successful in making distinctions about. For example, if the student doesn't yet grasp the concept of living and non-living things, they might make distinctions by color. If the student isn't well-versed in parts of speech, they might make distinctions between words with and without a suffix.

◆ Have students store their Distinction Pockets in a three-ring binder to use in future lessons.

Cause/Effect Dominoes

Cause/effect relationships can be simple or very complex. Many students grasp the notion that one thing leads to another, but struggle with the more abstract idea of a chain or domino effect. Research shows that tactile manipulation can boost understanding of abstract or complex ideas. By combining a teacher-made version of dominoes with text-based information, students can manipulate the cause/effect chain for a deeper, more memorable understanding.

Selected IEP goal

◆ *Describe the connections between a series of events…*

Other possible IEP goals:

◆ Make logical predictions…
◆ Describe how his behavior affects others…
◆ Apply personal safety measures in a variety of situations…
◆ Develop a personal budget…

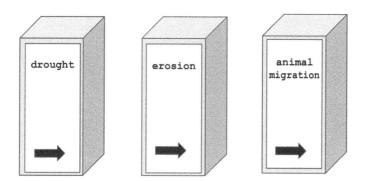

Figure A.2 Cause/Effect Dominoes

How to:

1. Obtain at least six small (1 ½ in. × 5 ½ in.) cardboard bakery boxes from a local bakery or grocery store. Any size will work as long as they are all the same.

2. Cut and laminate pieces of white card stock approximately 1 ¼ in. × 5 in. and adhere them to one edge of each box as in Figure A.2.

3. Show the student a short video of the domino effect, such as https://www.youtube.com/watch?v=dWp0VQRUyP4&t=11s

4. Explain that a cause has an effect, but that often that effect becomes a cause of something else. This chain reaction can be seen in text when an author shares a series of events.

5. Provide the student with a text that includes a series of cause/effect events and have them read it or listen to it.

6. After a first read through, ask the student to identify one thing that occurred. Use a water-based or dry-erase marker to write that event on one of the dominoes. Draw an arrow underneath it facing to the right.

7. Ask the student to identify one of the effects of the first event, and write it on a second box, including another arrow facing to the right. Line this up near the first box

8. Continue in this fashion until all of the chain is represented on the boxes and you have several lined up in domino style. Reread the text as necessary to capture several of the events.

9. Direct the student to gently tap the first box (cause) so that it knocks into the second and starts the dominoes to collapse in sequence. Explain how this cause/effect chain occurs in so many of life's experiences and generate other examples with the student.

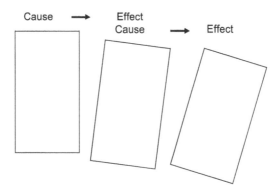

Figure A.3 Cause/Effect Graphic Organizer

10 As your progress monitoring data begins to show student growth, develop a plan to fade to a two-dimensional graphic organizer such as the one shown in Figure A.3.

Other considerations:

◆ For some students it will be beneficial to practice predicting a chain of events as a pro-active decision-making strategy. For example, have a student predict the effects of walking away from a student who is annoying them rather than engaging in conflict. By exploring various examples, students are developing their executive function skills of response inhibition and self-regulation.

Check Box Strategy

Many students with disabilities struggle with lengthy, multi-step directions. They may start off correctly, but then skip a step or two, or hand in incomplete work. This is especially problematic when students must comprehend and follow test directions on their own for high-stakes tests. The Check Box Strategy helps students chunk, plan, execute and evaluate the completeness of their responses to multi-step directions.

Selected IEP Goal: *Utilize test-taking strategies to comprehend directions and monitor work accuracy…*

Other possible IEP goals:

◆ Restate key details of a text …
◆ Follow simple written recipes…

- ◆ Review work for accuracy and make necessary corrections...
- ◆ Sequence a series of events or steps

How to:

1. Provide the student with a print version of a lengthy, multi-step direction. It is best if it is an authentic task.
2. Place a copy of the directions under your document camera and project to the class so that you can model the strategy.
3. Tell students that you will be teaching them the Check Box Strategy, placing boxes wherever specific tasks are mentioned. Explain that as they go through the tasks, they will be able to check them off it ensure that they have completed everything that was required.
4. Ask students to read along. Stop whenever a "to do" or task arises and model how to place a small check box over the direction. Continue modeling two or three times.
5. Direct students to read the next few sentences and talk with peers about where they think they should put check boxes.
6. Bring students back together to share ideas and discuss. Students frequently disagree about how many check boxes to include. Even though there may not be one and only one correct answer, guide students to make decisions that will lead to the best outcome.

Other considerations:

- ◆ Taking assessments in a digital environment? Tweak this strategy by having students make a numbered list on scrap paper, drawing a box next to each number and writing a word or phrase that captures the idea of the task. They can then check these off as they complete the tasks.

Close Your Eyes and Visualize Strategy

Attending to details in a story helps a reader to visualize the setting, characters and plot, improving overall comprehension. Adding these details to writing paints a clear picture for our reading audience. In both reading and writing, research shows that practice with visualization can improve these skills.

Selected IEP Goal: *Write about an event, including details and elaboration to describe nouns and verbs*

Other possible IEP goals:

◆ Identify possible consequences of two different actions
◆ Follow directions related to job requirements
◆ Anticipate and prepare for efficient transitions between daily activities (Figure A.4)

How to:

1 Obtain a Director's Clapboard (available online) or make one out of cardboard.
2 Show it to the student(s) and explain how a writer and a movie director have to clearly describe what they want their set and costume designers and actors to do before they begin filming.
3 Teach the student(s) to chant, "Close your eyes and visualize." Explain that they will repeat that phrase when they hear you clap the board, and then close their eyes to picture an image as you read aloud some text.
4 Once the student(s) has their eyes closed, read the following sentence aloud – "The firefighter went down the hall."
5 Direct them to open their eyes. Ask the following questions and allow for discussion.
    ◆ Did you picture a man or a woman?
    ◆ Was the firefighter wearing a uniform?
    ◆ Where was the hall you pictured? At school? An office? A home?
    ◆ Did you see smoke or flames?
    ◆ Did you hear noise?

Figure A.4 Director's Clapboard

6 Explain that the original sentence didn't have any of these details, so it could have been a female firefighter in her pajamas walking from her bedroom to her kitchen. It is the details that make the story.

7 Work together to create a more detailed sentence about the firefighter.

8 Repeat as desired with additional sentences lacking detail.

9 Direct the student(s) to find a sentence in their own writing that could benefit from extra detail. Ask them to "Close your eyes and visualize" prior to editing.

Other considerations:

◆ For a more rigorous twist, ask students to work backwards by taking a detailed sentence, removing all of the description until just the skeleton is left. Discuss the differences.

Streamlined Steps Strategy

Identifying your metacognitive process yields a powerful personal awareness that can often be translated into actionable ideas for students. When faced with complex directions in mathematics, science or any content area, I reflect on my own thinking. What do I do to be successful? Many adults subconsciously try to turn the directions into numbered steps, sometimes jotting them down and adding icons to help with understanding and memory. Providing students with explicit instruction in this process gives them a generalizable, life-long learning skill.

Selected IEP goal

◆ *Solve addition and subtraction word problems...*

Other possible IEP goals:

◆ Activate and utilize an alternative communication device with peers
◆ Identify public transportation route by using a map
◆ Write an opinion piece with reasons to support claim
◆ Graph functions showing key features

How to:

1 Activate the student's prior knowledge of delineating steps by discussing several examples that will be familiar to them. For example, perhaps you have taught the student three steps to cross the street or four steps for self-regulation.

```
1.Who has the most?
2.The one with more goes on top.
3.Read and highlight or circle key words.
4.Fill in the rectangle and oval.
5.Solve the problem.
```

1.Who   ☺ ?

2.More on top   ▽

3.Read + mark   ◯

4.Fill   ▼

5.Solve   1+1=?

Figure A.5 Streamlined Steps Example

2   Explain that in math, there are many times when teachers present a task with multiple steps. As they are talking, it can help to figure out how to streamline the steps for yourself.

3   Model using a familiar math process or use the following example about comparison bars for solving addition and subtraction story problems. Begin by giving the directions in a lecture or monologue form.

4   Show the student how those directions can be turned into simpler steps such as in Figure A.5.

5   Discuss with the student how steps can be streamlined even further by looking for key words, as in Figure A.5.

6   Use a "we do" approach to choose images with the student to add to each step for additional cuing, as in Figure A.5.

7   Direct the student to follow the streamlined steps with a word problem to see if the steps are effective and efficient. Guide the student to reflect – Is there anything they would like to change?

8   Practice steps 4–7 until data show that the student has become skilled at using the Streamlined Steps Strategy in math. If this same strategy might be helpful in other content areas, design and implement a generalization plan.

Flip the Focus for Inferencing

We have a solid evidence base that shows inferencing skills can be enhanced by helping students to focus on missing pieces. However, many students are taught to make inferences by focusing on context clues that are present. By flipping the focus, we offer students an adapted method that might work better for them. This lesson example includes multiple layers of scaffolding so that students can feel successful with each small step, building their inferencing skills as they go along.

Selected IEP Goal: *Infer meaning from text using past experience and contextual clues...*

Other possible IEP goals:

◆ Analyze images and text for details
◆ Make connections to own life
◆ Improve problem-solving skills in a variety of unexpected situations
◆ Identify common objects and colors when presented with images

How to:

1 Find at least six intriguing photos that will capture a student's interest. Cut away half of three of the photos, so that the student will only see half (Figure A.6).
2 Compose several sentences, some with missing information.

Figure A.6 Photo Examples

3   Begin by showing a full image to a student and modeling a think aloud, showing how to make an inference about the picture. Ask yourself questions out loud, such as "How do I know?" "What life experience helps me think this?"

4   Ask the student to make inferences about the two remaining whole images, using the same questions.

5   Show the student a half-image and model a think aloud, as in Step 2, but inserting the question "What's missing?" at the beginning.

6   Ask the student to make inferences about the two remaining half-images, using the series "What's missing?" "How do I know?" "What life experience helps me think this?"

7   Present the student with a full sentence such as
      Everyone "oohed" and "ahhed" as the sky lit up, but the dogs barked with each loud bang.
      In the kitchen, Luis was looking at his feet as his mother held up the broken pieces.

8   Direct the student to make inferences about the complete sentences, modeling and prompting as necessary with "How do I know?" "What life experience helps me think this?"

9   Present the student with a partial sentence such as
      Yasmine was _____ as her mother tried to comfort her.
      The wind was so strong that the tree _____.

10 Guide them to ask, "What's missing?" "How do I know?" "What life experience helps me think this?" with each sentence.

Other considerations:

◆   Increase the rigor by moving to paragraphs and asking students to generate additional questions, as in the following example:
      When I got to school this morning, all of the teachers were hurrying around to get us ready to leave. "Did you all put your lunches in the cooler? If you brought sunscreen, please bring it to me." The teachers are checking their lists and making sure we have everything we need.

Questions students might generate:

◆   Why are teachers hurrying?
◆   Where are they going?
◆   What will the weather be like?
◆   Will they be inside or outside?

Prior Knowledge Spinners

Successful learners manage to activate their prior knowledge on a topic before responding to questions or a prompt. Making these connections has been shown to be a highly effective practice. While many people accomplish this at a subconscious level in a split-second of time, others need to be taught a structure to use. The Prior Knowledge Spinner Strategy helps students to be more aware of the process and have a structure they can generalize to many settings and tasks. Rather than saying "I don't know" students can access whatever they do already know that might be relevant.

Selected IEP Goal: *Activate and describe prior knowledge of a previously learned topic…*

Other possible IEP goals:

◆ Relate text to other life experiences or texts
◆ Use effective search terms to locate relevant information
◆ Choose from three strategies to solve a real-world math problem
◆ Formulate and answer questions involving data charts

How to:

1   Make a copy of the Prior Knowledge Spinner in Figure A.7.
2   Provide the student with a paperclip to use as the spinning center and a pencil to hold it in place.
3   Model by posing a topic you know little about, e.g. coding. Spin and ask whichever question arises. For example, if it lands on "Who," I might ask "Who do I know that might know about coding." If it lands on "Where," I might ask "Where might have I learned about coding before?" Each of these questions may open memory paths that will provide some prior knowledge to use in the answer.
4   Provide a topic to the student and ask them to spin, answering each question to the best of their ability. Explain that if the first question doesn't activate sufficient prior knowledge, one of the others will.
5   Fade the use of the paper spinner over time, encouraging students to use the six question words to activate their prior knowledge. Practice as often as necessary so that the student becomes independent and can generalize the skill to different tasks and settings.

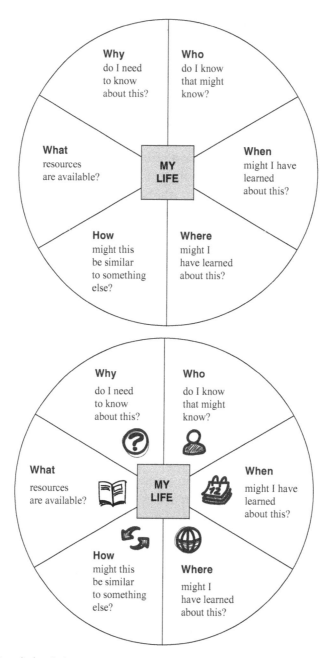

Figure A.7 Prior Knowledge Spinner

Scaffolded Summarization with Sticky Notes

Active summarization has been proven to boost learners' comprehension and memory. This no-prep strategy teaches students how to quickly review, highlight key ideas and summarize their learning. Best used after brief chunks of information, frequent practice will help the student remember the strategy when they are working independently in other settings.

Selected IEP goal: *Identify main ideas in a brief summary...*

Other possible IEP goals:

◆ Choose and use study strategies to assist in memorizing new information
◆ Synthesize multiple ideas into a written conclusion
◆ Follow multi-step directions
◆ Actively self-monitor comprehension of text

How to:

1 Choose an interesting three-paragraph text at the student's reading level.
2 Provide the student with sticky notes
3 Read the first paragraph aloud and perform a think aloud about how to summarize the main idea in five words or less. Write the words on a sticky note and stick in the margins next to the paragraph (Figure A.8).
4 Guide the student to read the second paragraph and then work together to summarize in five words or less.
5 Ask the student to do the third paragraph independently. Provide appropriate feedback.

Figure A.8 Summarization with Sticky Notes

6 Direct the student to reread all three sticky notes in order. Model how to combine the three ideas into one summary statement.
7 Repeat the process with other texts, gradually reducing the support. Add longer texts as the student becomes more successful.

Other considerations:

◆ If the student is reading a digital text, show them how to make notations in the margin.
◆ Not all digital texts will allow for annotations, especially during standardized testing. Teach the student how they can make a numbered list on scrap paper and jot down their brief summaries.

Bibliography

Agarwal, P., H. Roediger, M. McDaniel and K. McDermott. 2017. *How to use retrieval practice to improve learning*. St. Louis: Washington University in St. Louis.

Amabile, T. and S. Kramer. 2011. *The progress principle: Using small wins to ignite joy, engagement and creativity at work*. Boston: Harvard Business School Publishing.

Anderson, M. C., & K. W. Thiede. 2008. Why do delayed summaries improve metacomprehension accuracy? *Acta Psychologica* 128:110–118.

Andreatta, B. 2018. *Wired to connect: The brain science of teams and a new model for creating collaboration and Inclusion*. Santa Barbara: 7th Mind Publishing.

Archer, L. Bruce. 1965. *Systematic method for designers*. Council of Industrial Design: H.M.S.O.

Bender, L., G. Walia, K. Kambhampaty, K. Nygard and T. Nygard. 2012. *Social sensitivity and classroom team projects: An empirical investigation*. Paper presented at the 43rd ACM technical symposium on Computer Science Education.

Beninghof, A. 2020. *Co-teaching that works: Structures and strategies for maximizing student learning*. San Francisco: Jossey-Bass.

Beninghof, A. 2015. To clone or not to clone? *Educational Leadership* 73(4):10–15.

Beninghof, A. and A. L. Singer. 1995. *Ideas for inclusion: The school administrator's guide*. Longmont, CO: Sopris West.

Bergeson, J. 2012. *Vitamin D for data: A prescription for marketing health*. https://www.business2community.com/marketing/vitamin-d-for-data-a-prescription-for-marketing-health-0200233

Berk, L.E. 2003. *Child development*. Boston: Allyn and Bacon.

Brown, P., H. Roediger and M. McDaniel. 2014. *Make it stick: The science of successful learning*. Boston: Belknap Press.

Center on the Developing Child at Harvard University. 2011. Building the brain's "air traffic control system": How early experiences shape the development of executive function. *Working Paper No. 11*. https://46y5e-h11fhgw3ve3ytpwxt9r-wpengine.netdna-ssl.com/wp-content/uploads/2011/05/How-Early-Experiences-Shape-the-Development-of-Executive-Function.pdf

Dawson, P. and R. Guare. 2018. *Executive skills in children and adolescents: A practical guide to assessment and intervention*. New York: The Guilford Press.

DeStefano, H. H. 2019. Learning targets: Helping kindergarteners focus on letter names and sounds. *Young Children* 74(5):75.

Donnellan, A. M. 1984. The criterion of the least dangerous assumption. *Behavioral Disorders* 9(2):141–150.

Duhigg, C. 2016. What Google learned from Its quest to build the perfect team. *New York Times Magazine,* February 25. https://www.nytimes.com/2016/02/28/magazine/what-google-learned-from-its-quest-to-build-the-perfect-team.html

Endrews, F. vs. Douglas County Supreme Court Decision, October 2016 p. 3 https://www.supremecourt.gov/opinions/16pdf/15-827_0pm1.pdf

Field, J. *The science behind guilt and shame.* May 15, 2017. https://themonkeytherapist.com/science-behind-guilt-shame/

Fowler, S. 2013. *Why motivating people doesn't work...and what does.* San Francisco: Berrett-Koehler.

Freedman, S. 2008. Define your personal leadership vision. *Harvard Business Review.* https://hbr.org/2008/08/title#:~:text=Leadership%20vision%20is%20an%20essential,and%20what%20you%20stand%20for.

Gonzalez, J. 2015. *Cult of pedagogy, Big list of class discussion strategies.* https://www.cultofpedagogy.com/speaking-listening-techniques/

Goran, L., E. Harkins Monaco, M. Yell, J. Shriner and D. Bateman. 2020. Pursuing academic and functional advancement: Goals, services and measuring progress. *Teaching Exceptional Children.* May 8. https://doi.org/10.1177%2F0040059920919924

Guskey, T. 2007. The rest of the story. *Educational Leadership* 65(4):28.

Guskey, T. 2003. How classroom assessments improve learning. *Educational Leadership* 60(5):8.

Hammond, Z. 2020. The power of protocols for equity. *Educational Leadership* 77(7):45–50.

Hattie, J. 2012. *Visible learning for teachers: Maximizing impact on learning.* New York: Routledge.

Hoover, J. and J. Patton. 2017. *IEPs for ELs and other diverse learners.* Thousand Oaks, CA: Corwin

Hutchins, K. 2018. *How to use videos to teach social cognition.* December. https://theschoolslp.com/mr-bean-social-thinking-videos/

Indiana Department of Education. 2018. *Spread the word. Considerations for specially designed instruction.* January. https://www.doe.in.gov/sites/default/files/specialed/specially-designed-instruction.pdf

Jackson, R. 2011. *How to motivate reluctant learners.* Alexandria: ASCD.

Johnson, N. and A. Parker. 2013. Effects of wait time when communicating with children who have sensory and additional disabilities. *Journal of Visual Impairment and Blindness* 107(5):363–374.

Jones, J. 2020. *SchoolX: How principals can design a transformative school experience for students, teachers, parents – and themselves.* Woodbridge: John Catt Educational.

Lin, X., D. Schwartz and G. Hatano. 2005. Toward teachers' adaptive metacognition. *Educational Psychologist* 40(4):245–255.

Marsalis, W. 2006. *How I work*. https://money.cnn.com/magazines/fortune/fortune_archive/2006/03/20/8371781/index.htm

Marzano, R. 2007. *The art and science of teaching: A comprehensive framework for effective instruction*. Alexandria: ASCD.

Marzano, R. and D. Pickering. 2010. *The highly engaged classroom*. Bloomington: Marzano Resources.

McClelland, M.M., C.E. Cameron, C.M. Connor, C.L. Farris, A.M. Jewkes and F.J. Morrison, 2007. Links between behavioral regulation and preschoolers' literacy, vocabulary, and math skills. *Developmental Psychology* 43(4):947–959.

McLeskey, J., M-D. Barringer, B. Billingsley, M. Brownell, et al. 2017. *High leverage practices in special education*. Arlington: Council for Exceptional Children and CEEDAR Center.

Moore, C., L. Garst, and R. Marzano. 2018. *3 types of learning targets*. https://www.marzanocenter.com/3-types-of-learning-targets/

Moss, C. and S. Brookhart. 2012. *Learning targets: Helping students aim for understanding in today's lesson*. Alexandria: ASCD.

Nawaz, S. 2020. To achieve big goals, start with small habits. *Harvard Business Review Online*. January. https://hbr.org/2020/01/to-achieve-big-goals-start-with-small-habits

Onosko, J. 1992. Exploring the thinking of thoughtful teachers. *Educational Leadership*. 49(7):40–43.

Poth, R. 2019. *Getting smart. Metacognition and why it matters in education*. https://www.gettingsmart.com/2019/10/metacognition-and-why-it-matters-in-education/

Prytula, M. 2012. Teacher metacognition within the professional learning community. *International Education Studies* 5(4):112–121.

Public Schools of North Carolina. 2019. *Educating the whole child: Considerations for specially designed instruction*. https://ec.ncpublicschools.gov/ConsiderationsforSpeciallyDesignedInstruction.pdf

Ralabate, P. and E. Berquist. 2020. *Your UDL journey: A systems approach to transforming instruction*. Wakefield: CAST.

Ralabate, P. 2016. *Your UDL lesson planner: The step-by-step guide for teaching all learners*. Baltimore: Brookes.

Ritchhart, R. 2019. Leveraging Culture: An interview with Ron Ritchhart. *Creative Teaching & Learning* 8(4):45.

Ritchhart, R., M. Church and K. Morrison, 2011. *Making thinking visible: How to promote engagement, understanding, and independence for all learners*. SF: Jossey-Bass.

Robinson, K. and L. Aronica. 2015. *Creative schools: The grassroots revolution that's transforming education.* New York: Penguin.

Rodgers, W. and M. Weiss. Specially designed instruction in secondary co-taught mathematics courses. *Teaching Exceptional Children* 51(4):276–285.

Rowe, M. 1986. Wait time: Slowing down may be a way of speeding up! *Journal of Teacher Education* 37:43.http://jte.sagepub.com/cgi/content/abstract/37/1/43

Schlechty, P. 2011. *Engaging students: The next level of working on the work.* SF: Wiley.

School Reform Initiative. *Protocols.* Retrieved October 1, 2020. https://www.schoolreforminitiative.org/protocols/

Schraw, G. and R.S. Dennison. 1994. Assessing metacognitive awareness. *Contemporary Educational Psychology* 19:460–475.

Sobel-Lojeski, K. 2015. The subtle ways our screens are pushing us apart. *Harvard Business Review Online.* April 8, 2015. https://hbr.org/2015/04/the-subtle-ways-our-screens-are-pushing-us-apart

Sprenger, M. 2018. *How to teach so students remember.* Alexandria: ASCD.

Tomlinson, C. 2017. *How to differentiate instruction in academically diverse classrooms.* Alexandria: ASCD.

Visible Learning Meta[x]. 2020.http://www.visiblelearningmetax.com/

Washor, E. and C. Mojkowski. 2014. Student disengagement: It's deeper than you think. *Phi Delta Kappan* 95(8):8–10.

Willis, J. 2015. *The anatomy of procrastination and how students can beat it.* October 21. https://www.theguardian.com/teacher-network/2015/oct/21/procrastination-how-school-pupils-can-beat-it

Wooley, A., C. Chabris, A. Pentland, N. Hashmi and T. Malone. 2010. Evidence for a collective intelligence factor in the performance of human groups. *Science* 330: 686–688.

Yell, M., D. Bateman and J. Shriner. 2020. Developing and implementing educationally meaningful and legally sound IEPs: Bringing it all together. *Teaching Exceptional Children* May 8. https://doi.org/10.1177%2F0040059920919087

Yell, M. and Rozalski. 2013. The peer-reviewed research requirement of the IDEA: An examination of law and policy. In Cook, B., Tankersley, M. Landrum, T. (Eds.), *Evidence-based practices* (1–26) Emerald.

Zak, P. 2017. *The trust factor: The science of creating high-performance companies.* New York: AMACOM.

Zeiger, J. 2014 *5 reasons why racing is easier than training.* September 8. https://racereadycoaching.com/5-reasons-racing-easier-training/#:~:text=A%20surge%20of%20adrenaline%20on,a%20pace%20you%20cannot%20sustain

Index

Page numbers in **bold** indicate tables, page numbers in *italic* indicate figures.

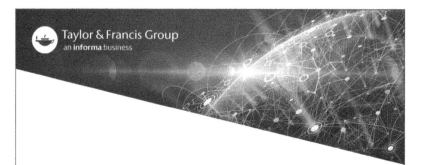